THE IDEOLOGY OF INDIA'S MODERN RIGHT

BY THE SAME AUTHOR

Human Rights and Terrorism in India

Ayodhya: Ram Temple and Hindu Rennaissance

Economic Development and Reforms in India and China

Hindus Under Siege: The Way Out

Sri Lanka in Crisis: India's Options

Terrorism in India: A Strategy of Deterrence for India's National Security

Rama Setu: Symbol of National Unity

Corruption and Corporate Governance in India: Satyam, Spectrum and Sundaram

Hindutva and National Renaissance

India's China Strategic Perspective

Virat Hindu Identity: Concept and its Power

Building the Sri Rama Temple in Ayodhya

2G Spectrum Scam

THE IDEOLOGY OF INDIA'S MODERN RIGHT

Based on

The Hindutva Mindset

Subramanian Swamy, Ph.D. (Harvard)

Member of Parliament, India
Former Union Cabinet Minister for Commerce, Law & Justice, India

HAR-ANAND
PUBLICATIONS PVT LTD

Reprint, 2024

Published by Ashok Gosain and Ashish Gosain for
HAR-ANAND PUBLICATIONS PVT LTD
E-49/3, Okhla Industrial Area, Phase-II, New Delhi-110020
Tel: 41603490
E-mail: info@haranandbooks.com/haranand@rediffmail.com
Shop online at: www.haranandbooks.com

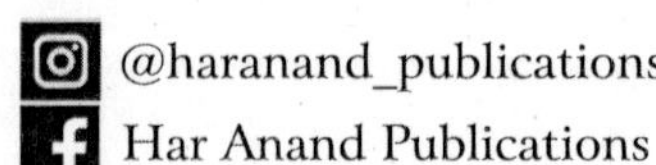

Printed in India

PREFACE

India, that is Bharat, and also known as Hindustan survived over 900 years of brutal foreign aggression of Islam and then Christianity, fought off cruel debilitating intrusive religious conversions and finally became victorious in 1947 overthrowing the foreign occupation and rule to emerge as a democratic republic of India.

Since then India has recovered substantially, remained democratic and survived five wars, suppressed secession attempts, and has now emerged as the third most prosperous country and second most populous nation in the world.

Today in 2018, India is at a turning point in history—whether or not it can emerge as a innovative global economic and military power with a population whose mental outlook or alternatively, the mindset, matches the requirements of this concomitant global role.

The answer in this book is: India must! That is, for the sake of global survival and stability in this 21st century. Whether we will rise to this commitment will depend on the appropriate commensurate mindset development of our people. This book is about how to structure that mindset development.

The overwhelming majority of India's population is the Brihad Hindu community—consisting of Sanatana Dharmis, Buddhists, Jains and Sikhs who together represent about 82.5% of the total Indian population.

India's religious minorities are constituted by Muslims [13%] and Christians [2.5%] and some other small religious groups. Though Buddhists, Jains and Sikhs are also considered minorities, they are really so close to the majority community in culture and indigenous ancestry that they are considered as partners of Hindu society.

Unlike Islam and Christianity, these other minority religions were born as dissenting theologies of Hinduism. They share the core concepts with Hindus such as re-incarnation, equality of all religions, and ability to meet God in this life.

That they feel somewhat alienated from Hindu society nowadays is the consequence of India's current identity crisis. The ideology of Modern Right seeks to end this current identity crisis and bring about a renaissance.

The ideological framework of Modern Right for achieving a national renaissance in Indian mindset, which I propose to articulate and propagate in this book in an intellectually challenging way, has the following markers:

[a] A social ethos, termed Hindutva or "Hinduness", based on the Hindu concepts of harmonious secularism, trusteeship of wealth, philanthropy, and voluntary group self help, for better quality of life, and for minimizing economic contradictions and deprivation.

[b] Hindutva flavoured state, based on the present Indian Constitution, minimalist in regulatory interventions in social and economic matters, maximalist in the maintenance of law and order, and in crushing terrorism and a governance which politically accountable to the people in a democracy.

[c] Empowerment of the individual through a modern accessible education that blends the essential concepts of spiritual commitment of Hindutva, with material pursuits, to

enable the individual to be self-reliant and have strong moral character.

[d] Actions of the State largely by incentives, and with exceptions, never by coercion. The state will make no promise to the people without specifying the sacrifice to be made.

[e] India's rapid economic progress with the goal to become an advanced developed country, as a globally competitive economy requiring assured access to the markets and technological innovations of the developed countries.

[f] A national security strategy for a peaceful environment which necessacitates strong security ties with such as of those countries with which India has no intrinsic clash of interests, principally the US and Israel, and harmonization of interests with China and Iran, and cooperative generosity in relations with Nepal, Bhutan, Myanmar, and Srilanka, and close cultural and economic relations with Hinduised South East Asia.

[g] A renaissance Indian, or Hindustani, transformed from one who presently has loyalty to the family but apathetic to the community where he lives; from one who does not easily acknowledge the accomplishment of others nor strives for competitive accomplishment; does not respect dignity of labour, and is more concerned with form than content in expression, and to bond with other Indians on an agreed common legacy and history.

[h] An Indian who feels accountable for his or her actions, and more so the higher he or she rises in authority. At present an Indian has character flaws that have come from two centuries of deprivation and are incompatible with a people seeking to emerge forming a great globally powerful united country.

These flaws can be rectified by developing a strong and coherent ideology of the Modern Right based on the concept of

Hindutva based national identity—whose defining characteristics can be culled from a correct perception of our Hindu history.

To propagate this new ideology I had founded the Virat Hindustan Sangam in 2014 (www.vhsindia.org). This book seeks to address a wider audience to make India a Virat Hindustan.

26 January 2018 SUBRAMANIAN SWAMY
New Delhi (India)

CONTENTS

CHAPTER 1

The Modern Right Framework

A constructive ideology of India's Modern Right is based on: (a) India's Constitutional Framework (b) Modern Hindutva imperatives and (c) Ancient Hindu Values and Governance Principles.

Hindutva is the quality of being a Hindu, namely "Hinduness" of a person's norms and beliefs as well as the code of good behaviour and civility, attributes that which would qualify and distinguish a Hindu from others.

India, that is Bharat, is the name of the Indian Republic as per the Preamble in the Constitution. The term Indian, that is Bharatiya, thus signifies a citizen of the Republic of India, which, as per Part II of the Constitution in Articles 5 to 11, defines the scope of Indian citizenship.

(a) India's Constitutional Framework

It is the task in this study to ideologically articulate the concept of the Indian Republic, re-interpreted in modern terms, yet within the Constitutional framework and in harmony with its time tested ancient Hindu ethos.

Today's India is the ancient Hindu nation, a continuing Hindu civilization in search of a renaissance, based on modernization.

Minorities need have no fear of this representation of modern India in Hindu terms, since the Hindu heritage means respect for the minority as demonstrated in our history with Syrian Christians, Arab Muslim traders, Parsis, and Jews. Parsis and Jews who were brutally persecuted elsewhere in the world by Muslim and Christian converts, but never in India where they lived in a safe sanctuary guaranteed by the Hindu community.

All these above named minorities have pursued spiritual aspirations and their goals of life in India without interference from the overwhelming majority Hindu community. Today they are protected by the Constitution of India.

(b) Modern Hindutva Imperatives

Modernization is mind development that takes place because of the stock of current knowledge absorbed through education, augmented by new research, and also learning by doing.

This knowledge is expanded and pursued with character that seeks to use knowledge to liberate and empower the human and not to enslave him. For this, religious philosophy has helped to develop character necessary for imbibing knowledge in an enlightened way.

India today leads the world in the supply pool of youth, i.e., persons in the age group of 15 to 35 years, and this lead will last for another forty years. This generation is most fertile milieu for promoting knowledge, innovation, and research. It is this prime work force that saves for the future and the corpus for pension funding of the old. We should therefore not squander this "natural vital resource."

Modern economic growth also is powered overwhelmingly (over 65% of GDP growth) by new innovation and techniques (e.g., internet). More capital and labour contributes less than 35% of growth in GDP. We must hence by proper policy for the young, realize and harvest the demographic potential.

The varna, or what in the West is termed as "caste system," was created to foster special classes, not birth based, to specialize in skills such as knowledge but to augment and research, military, wealth creation and agriculture.

Brahmins were venerated because they led a simple life and were devoted education and religious theology. That is, being Gyani and Tyagi as a pre-condition for their highest social status.

The "caste" system [i.e., Varna and Jati] was never meant to create a Brahmin hegemony or was conceived to be birth based. To become a *rshi* or *a sage* it was not necessary to be born of Brahmin parents. Valmiki, Veda Vyasa, Vishwamitra, and Kalidasa were not born in Brahmin families.

Nor were Brahmins above the law. Ravana, a Brahmin scholar of repute had to pay a heavy price with his life for his abduction of the wife of Sri Rama, a Kshatriya.

Varna identification instead was by gunas [virtues or qualities], as Lord Krishna told Arjuna according to the Gita. Krishna in the Bhagavad Gita says: '*caturvarnyam maya srishtam guna-karma vibhagashah*.' This means: "The four classification (varna) are made by me based on character (guna) and duties (karma)." In due course, this became perverted as 'caste' based on birth—which we hold today as a serious corruption of our dharma and a pernicious illegimate division of Hindu society.

Nor the recent researches on DNA of Indians show any racial differences amongst varna or jati i.e., castes, as alleged by British Imperialists and their brainwashed tutees in academics even today. Nevertheless, as a policy we must treat the stock of young population irrespective of caste as our potential demographic dividend.

China is the second largest world leader in young population today. But the youth population in that country will start shrinking from 2015, i.e., less than a decade from now because of lagged effect of their ill-thought one-child policy. Japanese and European total populations are fast aging, and will start declining in *absolute* numbers from next year.

The US will however hold a steady trend thanks to a liberal policy of immigration till recently especially from Mexico and Phillipines. But even otherwise the US will have in a decade hence a demographic shortage in skilled personnel.

All currently developed countries thus experience a demographic deficit. *India will not.* Our past alleged liability of fast growing population already second largest in size in the world, but by a fortuitous turn of fate has now become to be globally regarded as our potential asset.

The primary object of education thus was for preparing the mind in all its facets. This training of the mind and the process of thinking were considered as pre-requisites essential for the acquisition of knowledge. Today, the West has re-invented this concept in the development of the intelligence in seven dimensions-cognitive, emotional, social, moral, environmental, innovational and spiritual intelligence.

Thus, India has now become, by unintended consequences, gifted with a demographic dividend of young population. If we educate this youth to develop and attain a high quotient of *cognitive intelligence* [CQ] to become original thinkers, imbibe *emotional intelligence* [EQ] to have team spirit and rational risk-taking attitude, inculcate *moral intelligence* [MQ] to blend personal ambition with national goals, cultivate *social intelligence* [SoQ] to defend civic rights of the weak, gender equality and the courage to fight injustice, to protect environment, innovate new technologies, and nurture *spiritual intelligence* [SQ] to invoke the transformative power of vision meditation, and intention to access the vast energy the pervades the cosmos to do out of box research, then we can develop a superior species of human being, a modern Indian youth who can be relied on to contribute to make India a global power within two decades.

Computers may have high CQ because they are programmed to understand the rules, and follow them without making mistakes. Many mammals have high EQ. Only humans know to ask why, and can work with re-shaping boundaries instead of just within boundaries. Humans can innovate and create new tools not animals.

The human being is constituted by soul, mind and body and functions on his intelligence and power of discrimination (*vivek*). The main objective, in fact, of *Sanatana Dharma* is to unfold the tremendous multi-dimensional potentialities of human intelligence, step by step, from the outer physical body level to subtle inner mental to intellectual, and ultimately to the highest spiritual level, leading to Enlightenment and Self Realization.

The ultimate goal of human life is thus to experience a deep sense of fulfillment. All else e.g., position, purse, power, prestige, prize, profession etc., are at best, simply the means to that goal which fulfillment be achieved only by acquiring and cultivating the ingredients of Dharma because the human, unlike the animal, can reason logically deductively and inductively, to conceptualise, analyse, discriminate and then theorise.

Besides the eternal and universal human values and norms, *Sanatana Dharma* prescribes other tenets of human life as well. Sanatana Dharma has provisions as well for emergencies (Apatdharma) of different kinds. The Vedas are the basic and primary sources of Sanatana Dharma and are regarded as the roots of Dharma.

Sanatana Dharma as expressed in different parts of the Vedas, has prescriptions for individuals living in different roles, e.g. as a mother (Matridharma), a father (Pitridharma), children (Putri/Putradhrma), a king (Rajadharma), a Guru (Gurudharma), a student (Shishyadharma), a woman (Naridharma), a husband (Patidharma) etc..

There is thus no conflict or contradiction between Hindutva and Modernization. What needs to be discussed is how to inculcate Hindutva so that a modern mindset can be acquired and how the modernization process can be structured so that Hindutva dimensions can be imbibed through our educational and family systems.

(c) Ancient Hindu Values and Governance Principles

The value system that we seek to nurture today is on the basis of our ancient wisdom, to modernize and optimize our behavior for social and economic change, or in other words, the inculcate the quality of being a renaissance Hindustani, or or possessing the attribute modernised *Hindutva.*

Hindu value system is a balance between hard skills (such as learning arts and science) and soft skills (such as morals and spirituality).

Hindutva means that society adulates knowledge and places it in reverence above military power or wealth. Society thus is structured with those who are *Gyanis* and *Tyagis* at the apex of the Social Order.

We find these values conceptually elaborated by Lord Krishna in the *Bhagavat Gita* and the practice of it as propounded by Patanjali in his *Yogasutras*.

But we cannot simply read the texts and learn these gems of wisdom, because these have to be re-interpreted in the modern context by our spiritual gurus of today.

But three values [dharma] are core to a Hindu mindset or mental make-up:

First, God in Sanatana Dharma does not *favour* anyone as other religions propagate. What you get is based on the Law of Karma. If you pray to God for rewards very sincerely then he may re-schedule your good karmas but not erase your bad karmas. Its bad consequences will be postponed to later life. Of course unexhausted karmas carry over to next life. Prayers with deep sincerity also adds to good Karma.

Second, a value prescribed in the Gita, is that everyone born has complete freedom of action but that the fruits of those actions are determined by a calculus of accumulated past and present karmas, audited by God.

Third, the *Varna* social system has today degenerated into a birth-based oppressive cartelized system that requires to be repaired to bring it in consonance with its original meaning.

In its original pristine purity, Varna system was conceptualized as decentralization of power that is composed of knowledge, weapons, wealth, land.

The most important theme of Hindutva is the freedom of the spirit to inquire and the Law of Karma. Just as science insists on freedom in exploring the physical world, Sanatana Dharma embodies freedom in the exploration of the spiritual realm.

But to do so requires mental and physical discipline, and this the *yamas* and *niyamas* provide the code by which the freedom to attain spiritual enlightenment and bliss can be enjoyed. Karma empowers you to do good and be satisfied with results of your effort whatever it may be. This is the mindset of Hindutva.

But there is no reason now tolerate the present practice of the "caste" system which at the very least, is obsolete and a stumbling block in the way of Hindu unity.

We need to thus find a way to campaign for the abolition of the caste system so that we may achieve a renaissance in Hinduism and form a virat Hindu polity.

CHAPTER 2

Modern Hindutva Mindset

We have already defined Hindustani as one who is a Hindu, *or one who is not but acknowledges* that his or her ancestors were Hindus. He or she need not be a citizen of India to be a Hindustani.

This is the concept of our *Asmita* [identity]. The term Indian, that is Bharatiya, includes those living in India or living abroad as citizens of the Republic of India that is Bharat.

India has been known as Bharat in the ancient Hindu religious texts, since time immemorial [e.g., Rg Veda at 3.52.12, the mantra of Maharishi Visvamitra], hence the implication is that modern India is a continuing entity and not a new Republic nation that was formed in 1950, and distinct from our ancient past.

India of today is the continuation of the past and is the outcome of Hindus ultimate victory, however imperfect and truncated, over foreign Islamic and Christian proselytizing aggressors.

Indians are a people, hence, who have always constituted a nation, living in a geographical location spanning from Kashmir to Kanyakumari bound together in a continuing civilization of more than 10,000 years, a people who are mostly of Hindu religious faith and the remaining of those others of separate but equally respected faiths, whose ancestry scientifically determined in DNA and Genetic studies is however Hindu.

The correct perception is that Indians are a people who have always constituted a nation living in a geographical location spanning from Kashmir to Kanyakumari, from Attak to Car Nicobar, Diu to Dibrugarh, summarized in every Hindu prayer as "Asetu Himachalam," and bound together in a continuing unbroken civilization of much more than 10,000 years, of a people who are mostly of Hindu religious faith and of those others of separate but equally respected faiths, but whose ancestry is however Hindu.

That is how the word Indian has evolved. Arabs even today refer to Indians of all faiths as "Hind." Chinese from centuries have called us as "Yindu." China has always, and even now in all its Official publications, still refers to India by the name "Yindu Guo" which translated is "Hindu Rashtra."

"Hindu" is described in the Constitution [Article 25, Explanation II] as one who is not a Muslim, Christian or Zoroastrian.

This means that at present about 82.5% of the population of India are, according to the Constitution, Hindus including Buddhists, Jain, and Sikhs.

Zoroastrians also should have also been counted as Hindus on the same basis, since in the Rg Veda, a group described as Poru bear uncanny similarity to the Zoroastrians. The holy Gathas of the Zoroastrians are similar to the Vedas. The great sage Sri Chandrashekhara Sarasvati, Parmacharya of Kanchi Kamakoti Mutt supporting this view, stated Zarathustra originals from Saurashtra. Thus Parsis originated in Gujarat, went to Persia and returned as refugees, following Islamic takeover of Persia.

One version of the origin of the word "Hindu" is to trace it as the word derived from the *sandhi* of "Hi of Himalaya" and "Indu" of Indu sagar.

The mindset created by the British imposed system was that Indians should be obedient to an oppressive foreign ruler and have a deep inferiority complex about the British and thus accept passively the status quo of those in power. That system too is more or less continuing today in a different context.

This situation now urgently needs to change if our nation has to undergo a renaissance and achieve its potential. Our nation today has the world's largest number young persons below the age of 25 years which is now known as our potential demographic dividend.

If the nation is to reap this dividend then India's youth needs to mature into a dynamic, rational risk-taking, educated individuals with developed intelligence, and motivated to think out of the box to engage in research and develop essential innovations for national progress, and thus usher in the nation's rapid growth.

The youth also need to imbibe patriotism and spiritual values to put national interest above narrow personal and parochial interests and not consumed by greed and jealousy.

In a nut shell, the youth must be educated to understand his or her national identity and destiny, and develop not just cognitive intelligence as at present, but several other dimensions of this human intelligence.

Universities are green houses for our youth to find their roots and develop and flower their intelligence for pursuit of their chosen careers after graduation and to live a good family life in a vibrant democracy.

Unfortunately the educational system we have today is basically the same as designed by Macaulay in 1835, with intention to produce civil servants and clerks for the British to rule over the Indian masses.

Since 1947 we have merely expanded that design to learn by rote the cognitive sciences without developing a questioning mind and curiosity to seek ways to innovate for a better future. A secure career without risk is the goal of every student even today.

To understand his or her identity, the youth must know what their roots are. In particular, what is their affinity with other Bharatiyas and destiny of India. Thus, education must include tuition to make the youth aware of what is India and in which direction the nation must move.

At present, India's youth learn nothing on how to anchor their values, except on unthinking adherence to the Western or European mores.

Freedom Movement leaders such as Mahatma Gandhi, Sardar Patel, Netaji Subash Chandra Bose and Bharat Ratna Dr. Ambedkar had clearly wanted India after 1947 to develop, rooted in its ancient wisdom, language, and heritage.

But the direction in which Nehru steered the nation during the seventeen years as Prime Minister was towards continued imitation of the culture of the European, and develop the economy on the Soviet Communist model. This has today caused an identity crisis in the youth.

Since the world view of economic development has now completely changed. It is no more thought of as capital-driven or as labour driven as Karl Marx had argued, but as largely knowledge-driven.

For application of knowledge, we need innovations, which means more original research and in turn which needs more fresh young minds—the cream of the youth—to be imbibed with appropriate learning, emotional drive and striving at the frontiers of research.

This requires adequate empowerment of mental faculty endowed with multi-dimensional intelligence. It is not adequate merely to foster *cognitive* intelligence only, as universities are doing today.

The message of the Bhagvat Gita is that there are other dimensions of intelligences, and recognized now abroad as *emotional, social, moral, spiritual, environmental* and *innovational*.

Our vast youth population is our demographic potential dividend, that can be tapped for national regeneration only if equipped and enabled with the seven multi-dimensional intelligence.

For decades since Independence in 1947 we had been told that India's demography was the main liability, that India's population was growing too fast, and what India needed most was to control its population, even if by coercive methods.

I had challenged this view as long ago as 1972, arguing that population growth was not India's problem [Noted demographer, Dr. Ashish Bose of the University of Delhi had published in 1972 my research as a chapter in his book titled: *India's Population*, in which I had argued that the youth of India would if empowered with education be an asset to the country's development and not a liability].

I argued then that modern science, and through the scientific innovations of freshly educated research minded youngsters, can overcome the limitations of land, natural resources and production.

I had then also called coercive family planning as "an obsession of developed nations." But the negative view of population prevailed till the 'nasbandi' [vasectomy] fiasco of the Emergency in 1975-77, which forced Indian politicians to become less vocal about the need for coercive family planning. But the prejudice about population growth in India continues into the 21st century.

Globally, India today leads in the supply of youth, i.e., persons in the age group of 15 to 35 years, and this lead will last for another forty years. We should not therefore squander this "natural resource."

We must, by proper policy for the young, realize and harvest this demographic potential. China is the second largest world leader in young population today. But the youth population in that country will start shrinking in proportion of total population from 2015, i.e., less than a decade from now because of lagged negative effect of their coercive one-child policy.

Japanese and European total populations are already fast aging due to economic factors, and will start declining in absolute numbers from this year (2009).

The US will however hold a steady trend thanks to a liberal policy of immigration, especially from Mexico and Phillipines. But even then the US will have a demographic shortage in skilled personnel.

All developed countries will experience a demographic deficit. India on the other hand will have a demographic dividend for most of the 21st century if we empower our youth with multiple intelligences. Our past liability, thus by a fortuitous turn of fate, has now become our potential asset for the future.

Thus, India has now become, by unintended consequences, gifted with a young population. If we educate this youth to develop cognitive intelligence to become original thinkers, imbibe emotional intelligence to have team spirit and rational risk—taking attitude, inculcate moral intelligence to blend personal ambition with national goals, and cultivate social intelligence to defend civic rights of the weak; gender equality, the courage to fight injustice, the spiritual intelligence to tap into the cosmic energy that surrounds the earth, the environment intelligence to preserve the integrity of Nature, and innovational intelligence to transcend limitations of resources, then we can develop a superior mindset of the Indian youth who can be relied on to contribute to make India a global power within two decades.

The concept of identity for an Indian is an imperative for a nation in order to respond to challenges to its independence, culture and moral fabric.

A nation must be of citizens with high level of integrity and patriotism. Integrity implies the inner strength and equilibrium which enables one to meet with equanimity the victories and set backs of contemporary politics.

All who have been in public life know of those moments when the problems surrounding them appeared insurmountable, and their means to deal with them grossly inadequate.

There are times when darkness gathers such as during the Emergency (1975-77), and one despairs whether the dawn will ever break out. It is at such times that one has to call upon those inner reserves of strength and power with which every human being is potentially equipped but which requires a spiritual evolution to realise. Such persons are called "Virat."

Not everyone can be like that. But those who evolve to be so become time tested leaders of the nation and inspire the people to strive harder and sacrifice narrow self-interests for the larger good of the nation.

Hindutva or Hinduness thus envisages a collective mindset that identifies India as the motherland from the Himalayas to the Indian Ocean and with it's glorious past. However pious a Hindu is, however prosperous Hindu temples become from doting devotees' offerings, *it is this collective mindset of the people that matters,* and not the piety of the individual alone in that collective.

For that it is suggested that the religious minorities can join in if they are proud of the truth that they are descendants of Hindus.

Then our nation may be defined as Hindustan i.e., a land of Hindus and those others who proudly acknowledge that their ancestors are Hindus.

There are therefore eight components of the Hindutva induced mindset that the nation needs today:

First, India's Hindus and others must regard and foster the concept of the nation as the unbroken civilization of Hindustan; and their common history of endeavours, struggles, defeats and victories.

Ancient Hindus and their descendents have always lived in this area from the Himalayas to the Indian Ocean an area called Akhand Hindustan, and did not come from outside.

Second, Hindutva requires that national policies for development should synchronize and harmonize material goals with spiritual advancement, which is Deendayal Upodhyaya's Integral Humanism philosophy.

Third, Modern India is a Spiritual State that adopts the concept: *sarva pantha sama bhaava.* Hence the declaration in the Preamble of the Constitution that India is a Secular State should be replaced by that of a Spiritual State.

Fourth, a national law requiring prohibition of induced and collective religious conversion. Such a law will however not bar re-conversion to Hindu religion, or the return of any Indian to his or her ancestor's faith.

Fifth, that there is no theologically sanctioned concept of birth based social hierarchy. Varna never was conceived as birth-based in Hindu scriptures, but a choice that was subject to each abiding by the prescribed disciplines of that Varna. The present practice of birth-determined Varna is un-Hindu, and is excess baggage to be off-loaded and purged from the body-politic of the nation is the interest of a *virat* Hindu unity.

Sixth, all Hindus to qualify as true Hindus must make effort to learn Sanskrit and the Devanagari script, in addition to mother tongue, and pledge that one day in the future, Sanskrit will evolve to become India's link language since all the main Indian languages already have a large percentage of their vocabulary derived from or in common with Sanskrit.

To re-throne Sanskrit, Hindi, vocabulary should keep Sanskritising Hindi itself becomes indistinguishable from Sanskrit, just as Pali became two thousand years ago.

Seventh, Hindus must prefer to lose everything they possess rather than submit to tyranny or to terrorism.

Eighth, the Hindutva art of governance would be structured on the principles of Ramrajya and the tenets Arthsastra of Chanakya the Hindu must have a mindset to retaliate when attacked. The retaliation must be massive enough to deter future attacks.

These eight attributes constitute a mindset that a modern Hindu must have to be in a position to confront the challenge that Hindu civilization is facing from Islamic terrorists and from fraud foreign Christian missionaries, who unfortunately are also aided and abetted from within the country by confused Hindus.

Without such a virile mindset which is virat Hindutva, Hindus will be unable to confront the subversion and erosion that today undermine the Hindu foundation of India.

This foundation is what makes India distinctive, and hence we must safeguard it with all the might and moral fibre that we have. National renaissance flows out from that.

India today culturally is a Hindu dominant nation, albeit politically a secular Republic. But still, in the Articles of the Constitution, the Hindu cultural primacy, i.e., Hindutva is recognised.

The Hindutva flavour emerges in various Constitutional institutions such as Parliament, Supreme Court, etc, which have Sanskrit slokas as their motto, such as Satyameva Jayate, Dharma Chakra Pravartana etc..

The Official language Hindi has to be written in the Sanskrit script of Devanagari [Article 343], and where necessary, Hindi must augment its vocabulary *primarily* from Sanskrit language [Article 351].

Although it was a Constitutional mandate that while secularism and equality before law are a part of our core values, nevertheless the flavour and primacy for social and economic development of the nation is rooted in Hindu values.

This becomes clear in the Directive Principles of State Policy [Articles 38 to 51 and 51 A]. In the governance of the country these directive principles have to be followed, and it shall be the duty of the State to apply these principles while making laws [Article 37].

What are these Directive Principles based on Hindu values? Gender equality is ensured in education, employment, wages, and inheritance [Article 39], Panchayat system for village administration [Article 40], Uniform Civil Code [Article 44], Prohibition of liquor consumption [Article 47], Ban on slaughter of cows [Article 48], and Preservation of our rich heritage of our composite culture [Article 51A(f)].

It is obvious that these principles are all rooted in Hindu culture and constitutionally are the guiding directives for enacting laws.

Hindu theology also extols transparency and accountability due to the concepts *of satyam, shivam and sundaram,* and in the concept of *karma* which is nothing but a concept of accountability. The concept of *yama* and *niyama* define the code for Hindus, and constitute an ingredient of Hindutva.

The concept of our modern nation, thus, is rooted in our ancient Hindu heritage. India is a new Republic but also an ancient Hindu nation. Hindu civilization is the longest surviving, unbroken, continuing, and unique ancient culture.

The Constitution of a nation is the framework of principles, values, and canons on which the society's governance is rooted. It is either codified as a written document as in India and US, or unwritten and based on precedents as in UK.

From the Constitution flow the criminal and civil statutes which lay down the laws which the citizen have to obey, and the failure to do so invites sanctions and punishments that include imprisonment and/or penalties such as a fine. Enforcement of these statutes is the Rule of Law.

India is, according to the Constitution, a Union of States not a Federation of Provinces. Hence no state can secede from the Union, and no territory however small can be amputated out of India henceforth. States can be temporarily or partly administered by the Centre.

Thus, Article 356 of the Constitution allows the Centre to take over the administration of any State for a temporary period. Articles 247 to 253 empower Parliament to enact laws and establish courts to enable the central Executive to supersede the state's Executive in administering law and order. There is a central civil service and a central police force positioned in the states.

Thus, the essence or quality of the modern Indian

Constitution is unitary. We must safeguard this quality for our national integrity.

In our Constitution, the Supreme Court of India has perhaps a wider jurisdiction than the highest court in any other Constitution. That is, while citizen rights are defined by the Constitution, it is to be enforced and given content by the judiciary. The judiciary is neither subservient to the Government on the one hand nor to the people on the other. The judiciary therefore stands above the popular frenzy and the Government might.

As Parliament and Legislatures represent the Will of the sovereign people, the judiciary must represent the conscience of the sovereign people. One is secured by periodical elections, while the other is ensured by life-long training, character, and experience. These two uphold the constitutionality in the rule of law.

In order that the spirit of justice may prevail in the society, therefore a well defined Constitution and independent minded judges are as essential as the structure of Institutions, so that laws are understood and well-administered. Strong, impartial and capable judiciary is the greatest need of the hour today as we are passing through testing times globally.

The Constitution is a framework of rights and duties for the citizens. Basic human rights are fundamental rights, but these are not absolute, being subject to reasonable restrictions.

For example, the fundamental right of free speech and expression enshrined in Article 19(1)(a), is contrary to popular view, subject to reasonable restrictions prescribed by Article 19(2). Constitution thus recognizes no right as absolute.

The Hon'ble Supreme Court has laid down the test and scope of "reasonableness" in a catena of judgments [e.g., in

(1998) 8 SCC 227 para 13 page 233]. For instance to be a reasonable restriction, it cannot conflict with Article 51(c) of the Constitution under the Directive Principles of State Policy.

The scope of the fundamental right can thus be circumscribed by law passed by Parliament. Lack of understanding of this causes ideologues such of Marxism-Leninism, popularly known is Naxalism, which advocate secession, or to fanatic religious hate group leaders such as those propagating Jehadi Islam justify evil and violent practices against non-believers.

The concept of Fundamental Rights {Part III of the Indian Constitution} was not a legacy of allegedly 'humane' British Colonial legacy, as British historians claim.

The demand for constitutional guarantees of human rights by Indians was made as far back as in 1895 in the Constitution of India Bill, popularly called the Swaraj Bill, which was inspired by Lokmanya Tilak, one of the great freedom fighters and architects of India's independence.

This Bill envisaged for India a Constitution guaranteeing to every one of its citizens freedom of expression, inviolability of one's house, right to property, equality before the law, equal opportunity of admission to public offices, right to present claims, petitions and complaints and right to personal liberty. This the British rejected.

In the Madras Session of the Indian National Congress in 1927 it was laid down that the basis of a future Constitution must be a declaration of fundamental rights. But the British Government's Simon Commission in 1930 turned down the demand for fundamental rights on the ground that "abstract declarations are useless, unless there exist the will and the means to make them effective." So much for the British claim of the legacy left behind by them!

In 1952, the Supreme Court held that fundamental rights were within the power of amendment granted under Article 368 of the Constitution.

In 1965, though the question did not directly arise, the Supreme Court by a majority of three to two *reaffirmed* the view that the amending power could reach fundamental rights. Strong doubts were however expressed by two Judges, namely, Mr. Justice Hidayatullah and Mr. Justice Mudholkar about the amendability of fundamental rights.

But in 1967, the Supreme Court in the Goraknath case, by a thin majority of six to five reversed their earlier two rulings, and held that Parliament had *no power* to amend any of the provisions of Part III of the Constitution so as to take away or abridge fundamental right {AIR 1967 SC 1641}.

The Supreme Court held that a constitutional amendment had to conform to the provisions of fundamental rights just like any other ordinary law. Accordingly, if the constitutional amendment violated any fundamental right, it was unconstitutional.

Thereafter, a full Bench of thirteen Judges of the Supreme Court was constituted to consider the question of the validity of the Constitution (Twenty-fourth Amendment) Act. The case directly raised the issue of amendability of fundamental rights.

On April 24, 1973, the Supreme Court delivered its historic judgment in Kesavananda Bharati v. State of Kerala {AIR 1973 SC 1461} case. Six judges held that the power of amendment under Article 368 was plenary and was not subject to any implied and inherent limitations in respect of any matter, including fundamental rights.

Six other judges and the CJI held that Parliament could not, in exercise of its amending power, destroy or damage the basic structure of the Constitution by altering the essential features of the Constitution and that fundamental rights were essential features of the Indian Constitution.

Accordingly, a constitutional amendment which merely abridged a fundamental right with 'reasonable restrictions' was not unconstitutional, *but if it abrogated* a fundamental right, the Supreme Court would strike it down as unconstitutional.

Hence, by a majority of one, the concept of an *unamendable basic structure* of the Constitution came into vogue. *This is our first pillar of Constitutionality.*

Thus Part III consisting of Fundamental Rights became unamendable, and hence beyond any Parliamentary majority. Unless a revolution scraps the Constitution, it is now a permanent given in Indian affairs.

The fundamental rights incorporated in Part III of the Indian Constitution have a close similarity to the Universal Declaration of Human Rights, 1948. During the course of the debates in the Constituent Assembly, members had also referred to the Universal Declaration of Human Rights.

But in 1975, India experienced a threat to fundamental rights from a new angle—it's suspension. Prime Minister Mrs Indira Gandhi claimed that the nation was threatened by internal disturbance and declared Emergency under Article 352.

Part XVIII of the Indian Constitution deals with Emergency provisions that enable temporary suspension of fundamental rights. Article 352 had empowered the President to issue a Proclamation of Emergency if he was satisfied that a grave emergency existed whereby the security of India was threatened by war or external aggression or internal disturbance.

Since this last expression was vague and liable to misuse as was in 1975-77, therefore by the Constitution (Forty-fourth Amendment) Act, 1978 during the Janata Party rule, the expression 'armed rebellion' was substituted for the expression "internal disturbance."

While a Proclamation of Emergency is in operation. Article 359 empowers the President to suspend the right to move any court for the enforcement of fundamental rights.

The Supreme Court in its judgment in ADM Jabalpur V. S. Shukia (AIR 1976 SC 1207) capitulated and held that right to life and personal liberty was suspended during the operation of the Proclamation of Emergency and during that period, the writ of *habeas corpus* is not available. Only Justice H.R. Khanna disagreed. The subsequent Janata Party Government of Morarji Desai reversed that—

The framers of the Constitution of India also seemed to be aware of the Hindu heritage of India. A perusal of the final copy of the Constitution, which was adopted by the Constituent Assembly on 26 November 1949, is most instructive in this regard. The Constitution includes twenty-two illustrations within its main body. These illustrations are listed at the beginning of the Constitution. The illustrations are apparently chosen to represent various periods and eras of Indian history.

These illustrations have been selected to represent the ethos and values of India, which the Constitution seeks to achieve through its written words. The framers of the Constitution appear to have had no doubt in their minds that the Hindu heritage of this country is the ballast on which the spirit of the Constitution sails.

The emphasis of these illustrations is on those symbols that encapsulate the most significant and authentic moments of a nation's history. The personality of Shri Rama, the enunciation of the Gita by Shri Krishna, the valour, humility and service of Shri Hanuman, the teachings of Bhagwan Buddha and Mahavira, the emphasis on academic pursuits symbolized by the Gurukul and the University of Nalanda. These images may not be said to exhaust the Hindu heritage, but they do capture the essential concerns of the Hindu mind: struggle against the evil forces, dedication to duty without passionate attachment, service and humility, compassion and charity, highest importance attached to learning and academic attainments, freedom to hold diverse opinions and view points and an uncompromising spiritual eclecticism.

These are the virtues that the Constitution seeks to visually represent and legally enforce without favour and fear. The Constitution, it was intended, to represent Hindu ethos.

The illustrations selected to represent the 'Muslim' period *also* imply this intention: Only two illustrations have been selected: (i) A portrait of Akbar and (ii) portraits of Shivaji and Guru Gobind Singh.

From the whole range of Muslim themes, only Akbar is selected. Akbar come closest in his ideals and practices to what can be called the Hindu spirit: his relatively liberal politics, his reported refusal to make the Mughal state an instrument of exclusive Muslim hegemony, his relatively less hostile attitude towards Hindu religion, his refusal to treat Hindus as degraded dhimmies on account of religious belief. Akbar approximated to a certain extent the Hindu ideal of social and political behaviour and unsurprisingly found a place in the Constitution of India.

The other two men who represent the 'Muslim Period' are Shivaji and Guru Gobind Singh: men who fought the persecution and bigotry of the Mughal rule under the successors of Akbar, especially Aurangzeb. Akbar is chosen because he was liberal: Shivaji and Gobind Singh are chosen because they fought the oppression and cruelty of the Mughal state which was acting as the instrument of Islamic religious supremacy. They refused to recognize a political dispensation that functioned as an instrument for the fulfillment of Islamic religious agendas. They fought for safeguarding the dignity of their culture and religious values from the depredations of a theocratic Muslim state.

The three, Shivaji, Guru Tegh Bahadur, and Guru Gobind Singh represent the grand spiritual if secular, ethos of Hindutva. *The Constitution of India is cognizant of this fact. To this should have been added the Kings of Assam's Ahom Dynasty.*

The pictures chosen from the British period and the era of India's freedom movement are also unique. The former era is represented by Tipu Sultan and Rani Lakshmi Bai, both inveterate warriors against European colonial domination, warriors whose battles were not defined in terms of mere speeches and slogans but enacted within the context of blood and sweat.

Another figure chosen from the phase called 'Revolutionary movement for freedom' is Netaji Subhash Chandra Bose. One is compelled to ask the question: Why is Netaji chosen to represent the revolutionary movement for the freedom of India? The fact is that it was Netaji whose gallantry and dedication raised the morale of the freedom fighters and led to wider repercussion in other sections of Indian society. His courage, his sacrifice, his fighting spirit are the true values representative of the final assault of the Indian people on the edifice of colonial rule.

The only person chosen to represent the theme 'India's Freedom Movement' is Mahatma Gandhi, whose deep association with Hindu values, Hind Swaraj and Ram Rajya are no hidden facts. The Constitution of India thus seems to have chosen very Hindu icons to represent its ethos.

The 'aroma' of Hinduness or Hindutva mindset also permeates the most important constitutional and administrative units of the Indian state. Nowhere is it more apparent than in the august premises of the Indian Parliament—a house where matters of national concern are discussed and the fate of the nation is decided. The head of the Lok Sabha is the Speaker, and what we find inscribed holdly above the Chair of the speaker is the following: *Dharmachakra Pravartanaya* (for the turning of the wheel of righteousness). It is accepted by all that the notion of 'Dharma' is the most significant cultural signifier of the Hindu world. The rulers of ancient India had accepted the path of dharma as their area of political exertion and the managers of free India's politics accepted that notion by putting the *dharamachakra* on the national flag, and the related motto in the central place of the highest legislative body.

The Parliament of India bears prominent reminders of the prevailing nationally accepted Hindu ethos at many places:

(i) At door no. 1 is inscribed –

Lok Devarampatraarnu

Pashyema tvam vayam vera

[Open the door for the welfare of the people and show them the path of noble sovereignty]. Chhandogya

(ii) At the door of the Central Hall –

Ayam nijah paroveti ganana laghuchetasam

Udarcharitanam tu vasudhaivakutumbakam [Panchantantra]

[To think in terms of 'me' and 'others' in a narrow say; for the men of liberal character the whole world is one family].

(iii) On the dome near lift no. 1 –

Na sa sabhayata na santi vriddhah

Vriddhah na to ye na vadantidharmam

Dharmah sa no yatra na satyamasti

Satyamna tadyachhalambhyupaiti [Mahabharat]

[No assembly is a sabha which does not comprise elders; he is not an elder who does not speak according to dharma; no dharma survives without truthfulness; and every truth is necessarily devoid of cunning and deceit].

(iv) On the dome near lift no. 2 –

Sabha v na praveshtaya

Vakavyam va samanjasam

Abruvan vibruvan vapi

Narò bluvati kilvishi [Manusmriti]

"Either do not enter the sabha, or if your do, speak only according to dharma when you are inside it. Those who do not speak or speak untruthfully and unrighteously are partakers of sin."

These teachings—and there are many more—inscribed on the domes and walls of the Indian Parliament signify the values that the fathers of Indian democracy and parliamentarianism wanted to inculcate. It goes without saying that all the noble virtues included in the above mentioned aphorisms are derived from the Hindu heritage of India. The founding fathers seem to have found a deep consonance between India's Hindu ideals and the ideals of a modern secular democracy.

The impact of Hindu heritage and its value systems on the legal and administrative life of India becomes all the more apparent when one examines the core ideals adopted by various institutions. Some of the examples are as follows:

(i) Government of India - *Satyameva Jayate*
(ii) Lok Sabha - *Dharmachakra Pravartanaya*
(iii) Supreme Court - *Yato Dharmastato Jayah*
(iv) All India Radio – *Bahujanhitaya*
(v) Doordarshan - *Satyam Shivam Sundaram*
(vi) Indian Army - *Seva Asmakam Dharmah*
(vii) Indian Navy - *Shan No Varunah*
(viii) Indian Air Force - *Nabhah Sprisham Diptam*
(ix) Delhi University - *Nistha Dhriti Satyam*
(x) Life Insurance Corporation of India - *Yogakshemam Vahamyaham*

These are ideals of the Hindu world. They do not convey religious dogmas, therefore no rituals or gods are invoked in them; they are civilisational values whose sanction comes from deep humanism and a commitment to a righteous way of life.

They are noble virtues whose adoption was deemed to be relevant for the future of modern India's democratic polity. The Indian Constitution and the Indian polity pay their homage to the ancient value systems of the Hindu way of life, and Hindutva.

Thus the interpretations of the higher judiciary of the land, assigning the Hindu way or Hindutva to the centuries old socio-cultural underpinnings of India are not an exercise of mere juristic interpretation. It is more fundamentally the acknowledgement of those social, cultural, ideational and political norms that give the people and territory of India their defining identity.

Inspite of the currently fashionable denial by the purveyors of a warped secularism, the Hindu underpinning of India's milieu have been vested with great significance by the leaders of the freedom movement and has been subtly but insistently stated in the structures of the democratic institutions set up by Independent India. Our Constitution, our Parliament, our highest Judiciary, and other important organs of the state recognize most clearly that the ultimate normative sources of inspiration for shaping free India's destiny would remain the millennia old heritage of Hindu ideals and civilisational concerns.

The founding fathers of India's political regime seem to have no doubt in their minds that India can remain a pluralistic and democratic polity only to the extent that it adheres to the fundamental values of a democratic, polyform and pluralistic Hindutva.

So the question arises: Will Hindutva be a contradiction or violative of the Constitution? In other words, can Hindutva be incorporated by amending the present Constitution subject to the Basic Structure Rule?

I find from my research that most major Hindutva goals do meet the test of Constitutionality and hence need to be pursued even under the present Constitution. Of the decisions of the Supreme Court commonly referred to in this regard as "Hindutva decisions," the most important one is in *Manohar Joshi* [(1996)1 SCC 169].

In his election speeches Manohar Joshi, the winning Shiv Sena candidate had said that "[T]he first Hindu State will be established in Maharashtra." The High Court of Bombay set aside his election. But the Supreme Court restored Joshi's election observing that "a mere statement that the first Hindu State will be established in Maharashtra is by itself not an appeal for votes on the ground of his religion but the expression, at best, of such a hope."

The Court went much further and using the words "Hindu," "Hinduism" and "Hindutva" interchangeably observed that those terms were not amenable to any precise definition and no meaning in the abstract *would confine the term "Hindutva" to the narrow limits of religion alone*.

The Court further observed, "[T]he term 'Hindutva' is "related more to the way of life of the people in the sub-continent. It is difficult to appreciate how in the face of [prior rulings] the term "Hindutva" or "Hinduism" per se, in the abstract, can be assumed to mean and be equated with narrow fundamentalist Hindu religious bigotry...." (p.159, para 37).

Rule of Law which is governance based on citizens' rights and duties, is structured in the Constitution of a nation while the enforcement mechanisms are based on procedures set out in the Constitution [e.g., Article 226 and 32 on Writs] and statutes consistent with it.

The Courts provide as an independent judiciary, the interpretations of and direction to the State of the same by. In Hindu tradition, there is a highly sophisticated body of rules of interpretation and procedures prescribed in Jaimini's *Mimamsa* (in Sanskrit means "investigation") which sums up the general rules of *Nyaya*.

Can we blend Mimamsa rules into the Constitution? Yes indeed. Recently, a Supreme Court judge Markandeya Katju in open court suggested the use of Mimamsa rules to fill the gaps in the traditional western Maxwell procedures in our courts.

Thus, Constitutionality consists of the *quality* of the statutes, of enforcement procedures of rights and the performance of duties, in conformity with the provisions and principles of the Constitution. This quality can be imbibed by us from the glorious Hindu texts of Mimamsa and Vedanta. In the name of modernity, defined as by our elite as anything Western, we have shown scant regard for our ancient tradition of legal argumentation.

The Supreme Court on 18 December 2007 the UP State Agro Industrial Ltd case observed that the Mimamsa Rules of Interpretation (MRI) were still relevant and ought to be used in Courts alongside the traditional Maxwell Rules. Mimamsa Rules have been used by our *rishis*, since Jaimini wrote his Sutras, to resolve conflict between various Smritis. The Supreme Court applied these Rules to classify "animal driven vehicles" in their judgment.

A Bench of Justice Markandey Katju and Justice A.K. Ganguly in its order in another case said "It is deeply regrettable that in our Courts of law, lawyers quote Maxwell and Craies but nobody refers to the MRI.

Most of today's lawyers would not have even heard of its existence. Today our so-called educated people are largely ignorant about the great intellectual achievements of our ancestors and the intellectual treasury which they have bequeathed us."

The Bench said further: "the Mimansa Principles were our traditional system of interpretation of legal texts. Although originally they were created for interpreting religious texts [pertaining to the Yagya sacrifice], gradually they came to be utilised for interpreting legal texts and also for interpreting texts on philosophy, grammar, etc. i.e. they became of universal application.

Thus, Shankaracharya has used the *Mimansa adhikaranas in his bhashya* on the Vedanta sutras. There were hundreds of books [all in Sanskrit] written on the subject, though only a few dozens have survived the ravages of time, but even these show how deep our ancestors went into the subject of interpretation."

The Mimansa or the Purva Mimansa Rules to be exact, were laid down by Jaimini in his *Sutras* written around 600 B.C. That they are very ancient is proved by the fact that they are referred to in many Smritis which themselves are very old. Thus, the Apastamba Sutras copiously refer to Jaimini's principles. Since these Sutras are written in very concise form it became necessary to explain them. Many commentaries were written on them, the main ones being of Sabara, who lived around Second Century A.D., and Kumarila Bhatta and Prabhakara, who lived around the Eighth Century A.D.

Before mentioning some of the Mimansa Principles it is necessary to give a short background. Classical Hindu Philosophy has six schools (shatdarshan) all of which aim at Moksha (liberation).

Purva Mimansa is one of these schools, and according to it one can achieve Moksha by performing Yagya (sacrifice) in accordance with the Shastras.

The Shastras consist of Shruti and Smriti, the former being superior to the latter. Shruti consists of the four Vedas, the Brahmanas, the Aranyaks and the Upanishads. Brahmanas are treatises written in prose which prescribe methods of performing various Yagyas.

To every Veda one or more Brahmanas are attached. Thus, the Aitareya Brahmana is attached to the Rig Veda, the Taitareya Brahmana to the Black Yajur Veda, the Shatapatha Brahmana to the White Yajur Veda, and the Tandya Brahmana to the Sama Veda.

After Shankaracharya's historic victory over Mandana Misra, Purva Mimansa, as a philosophic system, declined in importance. Shankaracharya was a proponent of Uttar Mimansa (also known as Vedanta), according to which Moksha can be achieved by knowledge of Brahma.

Shankaracharya preached that Jnanakanda (the Vedantic Path) is superior to Karmakanda (the performance of Yagya).

He shifted the emphasis in the Shrutis from the Brahmanas to the Upanishads, and his view was accepted, and ever since Vedanta became the dominant school of Hindu philosophy.

However, though Purva Mimansa lost prominence to Vedanta in Philosophy, its importance remained as paramount as before in the legal sphere. It must however be clarified that the Mimansaks were not jurists.

Their aim was to perform the Yagya properly, for they sincerely believed that this was the means to achieve moksha. For the conduct of Yagyas in accordance with the rules they had to devise a system of interpretation to resolve the conflicts, ambiguities, etc. in the Shrutis, which were aggravated by the archaic, pre-Panini Sanskrit employed in the Vedic texts.

No doubt the principles of interpretation were initially evolved to resolve conflicts that arose in connection with the meaning of rules governing performance of the Yagya, but gradually these principles came to be accepted for interpreting legal texts also which were mixed up with religious rules in the Smritis.

It was therefore natural that our great commentators like Vijnaneshwara, Jimutvahana, etc. had utilised these Mimansa principles whenever faced with any ambiguity or conflict in the various Shastras. Unfortunately, there has not been much effort to explain these principles. The advent of Anglo-Saxon Law coerced on us must have been responsible for this lack of study.

The Mimansa principles are in two respects superior to Maxwell's principles of interpretation, viz.: (1) They can be utilised not only for interpreting statutes but also judgments, whereas Maxwell's principles can only be used for interpreting statutory law, (2) They are more detailed and systematic.

The Mimansa Principles distinguish between obligatory statements and non-obligatory statements. The main obligatory rule is called a Vidhi (or a Pratishedh, if it is in negative form). Vidhis are of 4 types, (1) Utpatti Vidhi, or a substantive injunction (e.g. 'perform the agnihotra'), (2) Viniyoga Vidhi, or applicatory rules (e.g. 'with curdled milk perform the agnihotra'), (3) Prayog Vidhi, or rules of procedure, and (4) Adhikara Vidhis (rules regarding rights and personal competence).

Apart from these Vidhis proper (mentioned above) there are also certain quasi Vidhis called niyamas and parishankhyas, but it is not necessary to go into details here. Vidhis are found in Brahmanas.

The main non-obligatory statement is known as an Arthavada. An Arthavada is a statement of praise or explanation. Most of the Vedas proper consist of Arthavadas as much of the Vedic hymns are in praise of some god, and do not lay down any injunction. Arthavada is like the preamble or statement of objects in a statute.

An Arthavada has no legal force by itself, but it is not entirely useless since like a statement of objects or preamble it can help to clarify an ambiguous Vidhi, or give the reason for it. Sometimes a Vidhi is also seen couched in the form of Arthavada. This situation has necessitated the need for evolving a system of interpretation. Six axioms of interpretation have therefore been developed for the interpretation of *shastras.*

By reason of the amendment of Article 359 of the Constitution by the Constitution (Forty-fourth Amendment) Act, the provisions of Article 21 cannot now be suspended or derogated from even during an emergency. No court can hereafter rule that habeas corpus is not available during an emergency.

The relationship of fundamental rights with the Directive Principles of State Policy in Part IV of the Constitution has been a subject of considerable and continuing debate. A division of fundamental rights into two categories—justiciable and non-justiciable - was recommended by the Sapru Committee as early as 1945. At the time of framing the Constitution, the Advisory Committee on Fundamental Rights recommended:

"We have come to the conclusion that in addition to these fundamental rights, the Constitution should include certain directives of State Policy which, though not cognizable in any court of law, should be regarded as fundamental in the governance of the country."

Directive principles are not enforceable by any court but the principles laid down are, nevertheless, fundamental to the governance of the country and it is the duty of the State to apply these principles in making laws (Article 37).

Part IV prescribes the goals or the ideals to be achieved by India as a Welfare State. Fundamental rights are the means for realizing these goals.

At one stage there was a sharp controversy regarding the role of fundamental rights vis-a-vis directive principles. Early judicial thinking took the view that directive principles were subsidiary or subordinate to fundamental rights.

The Constitution also prescribes the rights and duties of a citizen and it is the responsibility of the State to ensure the citizen gets his rights, as also encouraged to perform his duties as a part of the soft infrastructure of good governance.

The structure of our Constitution is consistent with the Hindu tradition, a part of Hindutva. Ancient Bharat or Hindustan was of *janapadas* and monarchs. But it was unitary in the sense that the concept of *chakravartin* [propounded by Chanakya], i.e., of a *sarvocch pramukh* or *chakravarti* prevailed in emergencies and war, while in normal times the regional kings always deferred to a national class of sages and *sanyasis* for making laws and policies, and acted according to their advice. This is equivalent to Art.356 of the Constitution.

In that fundamental sense, while Hindu India may have been a union of kingdoms, it was fundamentally not a monarchy but a Republic. In a monarchy, the King made the laws and rendered justice, as also made policy but in Hindu tradition the king acted much as the President does in today's Indian Republic.

The monarch acted always according the wishes and decisions of the court-based advisers, mostly prominent sages or Brahmins. Thus Hindu India was always a Republic, and except for the reign of Ashoka, never a monarchy. Nations thus make Constitutions but Constitutions do not constitute nations.

Because India's Constitution today is unitary with subsidiary federal principles for regional aspirations, and the judiciary and courts are national, therefore the Rajendra Prasad—monitored and Ambedkar—steered Constitution—making, was a continuation of the Hindu tradition. *This is the second pillar of constitutionality for us—the Hindutva essence*! These aspects were known to us as our *Smritis*. Therefore, it is appropriate here to explore ways by which Hindutva can be blend into the present Constitution more explicitly.

The Hindutva plank of restoring temples that were demolished by Islamic tyrants and mosques built on it, is constitutional thanks to the judgment in the Farooqui case.

In this case [(1994) 6 SCC 361], the Constitution Bench has held that a mosque *is not an essential part of Islam and hence it can be demolished for a public purpose by a Government*. This opens the way for building a Ram temple in Ayodhya. Of course, the 1992 demolition of the Babri Masjid would have to regarded as an offence under the IPC because of a mob taking law into its own hands.

But the Babri Masjid demolition offence does not prevent a future Hindutva government from demolishing Masjids and Churches (also not an essential part of Christianity) built after demolishing Hindu temples.

As the House of Lords U.K has held (1992) in the Nataraj idol case, because of *Prana prathista puja,* according to Agama Shastra, a temple is always a temple even if in disuse.

Thus for restoring the Kashi Visvanath temple or the Krishna Janmabhoomi temple, demolishing of the existing mosques by a government is constitutionally permitted.

Even in the Ramjanmabhoomi temple case currently entangled on the unauthorized demolition by some people taking law into their own hands, it is an IPC offence and has no constitutional significance. Any government can even now take-over the project for public good, and build a Ram Janma bhoomi temple.

Third, Article 370 is peculiar provision. It can be deleted, without a Parliamentary amendment, by a Presidential notification, subject to the concurrence of the J&K Constituent Assembly which however has long ceased to exist.

Moreover, the moral basis for it has eroded completely because the Kashmiri majority has already driven out Pandits completely altering the religious composition of the state, to preserve which the Article was incorporated.

Hence, there is no fetter now to constitutionally abolish Article 370 by a notification. By way of abundant precaution the President can obtain the concurrence of the J&K Governor who legally can be treated as a proxy for the J&K Constituent Assembly.

Since the Article 44 is a Directive Principle for State Policy to have uniform *civil* code and moreover since the Muslims on ground of violation of the Shariat have not objected to a uniform *criminal* code which the Indian Penal Code is, hence it is constitutional to enforce Article 44 as not violative of Article 15, since the latter is subject to reasonable restrictions of health, morality and public order.

The question whether India should adopt a uniform civil code should be treated as a legal question because it is a mandate addressed to the 'State' by Art.44 under Directive Principles of the Constitution.

Unfortunately, in India, legal questions are politicized when it affects the "Muslim vote bank."

Article 44 of the Constitution says–

"The State shall endeavour to secure for the citizens a uniform civil code throughout the territory of India."

A controversy has however arisen as to the formation of a uniform code relating to the family or personal law of the parties relating to matters such as marriage and divorce, succession, adoption.

The framers of the Constitution clearly indicated what they meant by the word 'personal law' in Entry 5 of List III of the 7th Schedule of the same Constitution.

Entry 5 says:

"5. Marriage and divorce; infants and minors; adoption; wills; intestacy and succession; joint family and partition; all matters in respect of which parties in judicial proceedings were immediately before the commencement of this Constitution subject to their personal law."

The fathers of the Constitution had witnessed the baneful effects of a claim for separate identity of the Muslim community on the ground that their religion prescribed a separate Personal Law,—resulting in the lamentable Partition of India on the footing of the theory of 'two Nations', founded on two religions.

Hence, in the Constituent Assembly it was made clear that in a secular State personal laws relating to such matters as marriage, succession and inheritance could not depend upon religion, but must rest on the law of the land. A uniform Civil Code was accordingly necessary for achieving the unity and solidarity of the nation. [K.M. Munshi, VII C.A.D., 547-48]. Every time subsequently the question of uniform Civil Code was raised by anyone in Parliament, the Government of India opposed it on the ground that to achieve it would be to hurt Muslim 'sentiments' and that no implementation of this Directive of the fundamental law could be made so long as the Muslims themselves would not come forward to ask for it. [see Prime Minister Rao Statesman, 1-6-1995; 28-7-1995], and also at his Independence Day Speech at Red Fort on 15-8-1995; Law Minister, Bharadwaj [Jugantar, 12-12-1993; Statesman, 22-7-1995]; Gadgil, Secretary General of Congress (I) Party [Vartaman, 21-4-1995]; Dinesh Goswami, Law Minister [U.N.I., 22-12-1989].

Nevertheless, the Supreme Court has recommended, more than once, to take early steps towards the formation of a uniform Civil Code [Mudgal v. Union of India (1995) 3 S.C.C. 635—Kuldip Singh and Sahai JJ. (10 May, 1995).

That the Shariat is not infallible or immutable is evidenced by the patent fact that it has been discarded on modified in many respects by various Muslim States. And this has been achieved in an orthodox Muslim State such as Tunisia, through the process of liberal or progressive interpretation of the scriptures.

Advocates of immutability should be silenced by the following observations of a Muslim Judge of Pakistan, Huq, J., of the Lahore High Court –

"it would not be correct to lay it down as a positive rule of law that the present-day Courts in this country should have no power or authority to interpret the Quran in a way different from that adopted by the earlier Jurists and Imams. The adoption of such a view is likely to endanger the dynamic and universal character of the religion and laws of Quran."

The ground of immutability of the Shariat was in fact raised by some Muslim members in the Constituent Assembly of India but was rejected on the opposition from Dr. Ambedkar. It would be an eyeopener to many today to recount what Ambedkar said [VII C.A.D. 55] in this context.

"... up to 1935 the North-West Frontier Province was not subject to Shariat Law; it followed the Hindu Law in the matter of succession and in other matters, so much so that it was in 1939 that the Central Legislature had to come into the field and to abrogate the application of the Hindu Law to Muslims of North-West Frontier Province and to apply Shariat Law to them ... apart from North-West Frontier Province, up till 1937 in the rest of India, in various parts, such as the United Provinces, the Central Provinces and Bombay, the Muslims to a large extent were governed by the Hindu Law in the matter of succession ... that in North-Malabar the Marumakkathayam law applied to all—not only to Hindus but also to Muslims."

Even in India the Koranic laws of crimes and evidence have been supplanted as early as the 19th century by enacting the Penal Code and the Evidence Act, e.g., by saving the Muslims from the following mediaeval atrocities which are still prevalent in Muslim countries like Pakistan and Bangladesh.

(a) Chopping off the hands of a criminal as a punishment for theft, or stoning to death as a punishment for adultery.

(b) Adultery and apostasy being punishable by death.

(c) Where the witnesses are women, their value as against the evidence of men is in the ratio of 2:1.

The entire law of criminal procedure has been replaced in India by statute. The Indians laws of crimes and evidence make no distinction between Muslims and non-Muslims. The Judges in a Muslim dispute need not be Muslims.

In this context, one critic has pointed out that in Goa, from the days of Portuguese rule, the people have been governed by a uniform civil code, but for the matter of that, Goanese Muslims have not lost their identity or culture.

If it is contended that personal law, founded on religion, has any special status, the answer is that it is the British Parliament which made the English Crown the head of the Church and altered the law of royal succession; and an Indian Parliament superseded the Hindu law of marriage and succession, in the teeth of opposition from an enlightened section of Hindus. It was opposed by Dr. Rajendra Prasad himself on the grounds that Art.44, being applicable to all persons in the territory of India, should not be imposed on the Hindus alone and that the Government who sponsored the Hindu Code Bill to replace the personal law of the Hindus had no mandate from the Electorate in this behalf.

Above all, the Muslims who remained in India after the Partition did so with the full knowledge that divided India was going to adopt a Parliamentary system of democracy and not any Muslim system of the Middle Ages where Shariat would be the supreme law of the land.

They should also have known that a personal law founded on the religion of different communities was incompatible with the very concept of a 'Secular' State which divided India was going to be.

Factually also, the assumption of the Government of India that the entire Muslim community is opposed to the implementation of Art.44 is not correct. The Shah Bano case demonstrated that it was only a section of the Sunni sect amongst the Muslims which was vehemently opposed to the judgment.

The Supreme Court can no more wash its hands off Art. 44 on the ground that it is a Directive Principle which is not directly enforceable. Jordan v. Chopra (1985) 3 S.C.C 62 Besides, some Supreme Court Judges had expressed their views to the same effect out of Court: Gajendragadkar, C.J., and Chairman, Law Commission, in his book—Secularism and the Constitution of India (1971), p.126; Shelat, J., Secularism, Principles and Application (1972); Hegde, J., in the Law Institute, in January, 1972; Tulzapurkar, J.,—article in A.I.R. 1987 Jours. 17; Beg. C.J., in his Motilal Nehru Lecture on 'Impact of Secularism on Life and Law.'

Prior to Kuldip Singh, J., in numerous cases, the Supreme Court has remedied the inaction of the Government in other clauses of Directive Principles to implement various Directives, in Arts. 38, 39, 39A, 41, 42, 43, by issuing 'directions' which are mentioned in Art. 32(2) as legitimate instruments in the hands of the Court.

Even in the matter of Art. 44, previous Benches of the Supreme Court had commented upon the inaction of the Government and the need for an early implementation of the Article –

(a) A unanimous Constitution Bench in the Shah Bano case (para. 32).

(b) A Division Bench, speaking through Chinnappa Reddy, J., in Jordan's case.

Today we have demonstrated by taking the "Teen Talaq" to Supreme Court and obtaining a judgment of the Constitution Bench that Teen Talaq is unconstitutional as vio; stove of equality before law [Article 14] and immoral [Article 25].

That the Shariat on personal law is not sacrosanct will appear from the following examples of Muslim majority countries which have superseded or modified polygamy.

Turkey: The Court can declare a second marriage as invalid on the ground that a spouse is living at the time of the second marriage [Turkish Civil Code, Art. 74].

Pakistan: A person cannot contract a second marriage without the permission of the Arbitration Council; and a wife can obtain divorce on the ground that the husband has married another wife.

Iran: A person cannot remarry without permission of the Court.

Egypt, Jordan, Morocco, Syria: Similar restrictions on bigamy as in Iran and Pakistan have been imposed in Egypt, Jordan, Morocco and Syria.

Tunisia: Bigamy is totally prohibited by the Tunisia Law of personal Status (s. 18).

Registration of all marriages, including those contracted in conformity with Shariat formalities, has been made compulsory in Iran, Algeria, Indonesia, Malaysia.

There is no reason why such law cannot be adopted in India.

Fifth, the call for Hindutva has been held by the Supreme Court in Manohar Joshi [1996] case to be within the Constitutional requirements of free speech. Hence, time has arrived for us to openly declare India as an ancient Hindu civilization, which is the only way we can perform the Fundamental Duty under Article 51-A(f), and boldly up revere our sacred symbols.

For example, the total ban on cow slaughter in Article 48 has been held by a 1958 Constitution Bench to possess constitutionality in the sense that the total ban is held to be a reasonable restriction on fundamental rights of all Indians.

At present the Government has been taking over Hindu temples its resources and land and using it for all kinds of non-religious purposes under the states enacted Hindu Religious Institutions and Charitable Endowment Acts on the pretext of maladministration of the temple properties.

Under Article 31A of the Constitution such a take-over cannot be permanent. If maladministration charge is true, then the Government should rectify it within a reasonable period such as three years, and then hand it back. At present State governments have taken over tens of thousands of temples for decades. Time is now to get them released.

These six constitutionally valid pillars are what Hindutva is, and it is significant that Hindutva goals can be achieved within the present Constitution.

Throughout ancient Indian history, Hindu kingdoms, never required any 'subject' to be of Hindu religion in order to be regarded a first class citizen. Only in Asoka's reign and Islamic rule, India was a theocracy. Hindu is naturally 'Secular'. But secularism is a much-bandied-about subject nowadays. Unfortunately, those political parties who have been swearing by it all these years have failed to persuade the masses that secularism is good for country.

In fact, secularism as defined and propagated today has lost its relevance. The concept as understood by the masses of India stands thoroughly discredited. Hence the question is whether we should redefine secularism in keeping our civilization tradition to make it acceptable to the masses or capitulate to the rising fundamentalism in the country with dire consequences for national integrity and security.

When Rev. Martin Luther had defined secularism in Europe, it simply meant that the power of the state would be exercised independently of the directions of the Church. Thus, a secular government would act to safeguard the nation-state, even if such action was without Church sanction. Later, Marx calling religion the 'opium of the masses' defined secularism to completely eschew religion.

In India, Jawaharlal Nehru and his followers subscribed to the later Marxist redefinition of the concept in which even in public functions, cultural symbolism such as lighting a lamp to inaugurate a conference or breaking a coconut to launch a project was regarded as against secularism.

This orthodoxy induced a reaction in the Indian masses. Nehru failed to define what historical roots ought to be a part of the modem Indian, and what was to be rejected. In the name of 'scientific temper', he rejected most of our past as 'obscurantism'.

His orthodox secularism sought to alienate the Indian from his hoary past. Since nearly 85 per cent of Indians are pan-Hindu in beliefs, and Hindu religion from its inception has been without a 'Church', 'Pope' or 'Book' (in contra - distinction to Christianity), therefore neither Martin Luther nor Marx made any sense to the Indian masses.

Since there was little political challenge to Nehru after the untimely death of Gandhiji and Patel, the Marxian secularism concept superficially prevailed till Nehru's demise in 1964. The masses therefore humoured Nehru without accepting his concept of secularism. A Conceptual void however remained to be filled.

But Congress Party continued thereafter to fail to provide a political concept of secularism by which an Indian citizen could comprehend how he should bond "secularly" with another citizen of a different religion or language, or region and feel equally Indian. The Hindu instinctively could not accept the idea that India was what the British had put together, and that the country was just an area incorporated by the imperialists.

Such a ridiculous idea, fostered quixotically by Jawaharlal Nehru University historians, found just no takers amongst the Indian people. The void remained thus, but the yearning in the masses to be "Indian" grew over the years with growth of mass media. This void had therefore to be filled and the yearning of national identity required to be articulated for the masses.

The legal perspective on Indian secularism has been brilliantly analysed by Supreme Justice Aftab Alam [in (2009) 10SCC J-60]. While he disapproves of the trends in, and import of the various Supreme Court decisions since 1994 as creeping Hindutva, I however welcome them. But I salute his research, which I have used in this Chapter *in fact to prove my point* viz., the Indian Constitution as increasingly interpreted by the Supreme Court is basically becoming 'Hindutva-friendly'. It has to be because the founding fathers of our Republic in the Constituent Assembly left no doubt that the Constitution was to be Hindutva friendly.

The Constitution of India recognises twenty-two languages as Indian languages. Indians speaking the same language may belong to different religions. India is home to eight major religions of the world. Conversely, Indians belonging to the same religious group may come from different parts of the national geography and may speak different languages, dress differently, eat different kinds of food in entirely different manners and may have completely different social and economic concerns.

In India, religion, a democratic State, and secularism overlap and combine to display a highly interesting and unique society.

India has survived while others with the same concerns have balkanized. But the important fact is that the liberality implicit in the Indian system is owed to the Hindu ethos of our civilization.

The Indian Constitution does not have any provision, unlike the First Amendment of the United States Constitution, proscribing the making of any law respecting an establishment of religion. *It instead recognises religion as a source of law.* With a view to protect minority rights, it confers affirmative social and cultural rights on religious groups. It guarantees the fundamental freedom of religion but enables the State, to regulate religious practices on certain limited grounds of morality, health and public order.

Thus, under the Indian Constitution, secularism of the State involves a plural establishment of religion with the State but maintaining of *equidistance* from all religions. The Court is called upon, in a variety of ways, to oversee and regulate the *distance* that the State ought to keep from religious establishments and the nature of State intervention permissible in religious affairs. *In that sense it would be more appropriate to designate India as a spiritual state rather than a secular state.* But confusion prevails today in the judiciary on how far to stretch secularism and how cognizant the law should be of the Hindu ethos of the nation.

For instance, keeping a beard by a Muslim student invoked Article 25 of the Constitution that gives to every person (in this case the Muslim student) the freedom of conscience and free profession and practice of religion. A Christian missionary-run school defended its rules not to permit it students with beards and expelled the Muslim student on the basis of Article 30 of the Constitution that gives to all minorities (in this case the Christian) the right to establish and administer educational institutions.

The expulsion was challenged unsuccessfully before the High Court and the matter finally came to the Supreme Court. On 30-3-2009 the petition was dismissed *in limine* but in course of the brief hearing, one of the judges made certain observations that were widely reported in the media. The Judge had said: "We don't want to have Talibans in the country. Tomorrow a girl student may come and say that she wants to wear a burqa, can we allow it?" [Times of India, March 31, 2009]. He further said: "We should strike a balance between rights and personal beliefs. We cannot overstretch secularism." Hence, the Judge added: "You can join some other institution if you do not want to observe the rules. But you can't ask the school to change the rules for you."

The remarks created an uproar among the Muslims against the remarks calling the beard and the burqa as the mark of the Taliban. Then, on 6-7-2009, on a review petition, the same Bench recalled its order dismissing the petition and requested the Chief Justice to have the case placed before some other Bench. On 11-9-2009 the case came up before another Bench. *And this time the response of the Court was completely different*: "How on earth could a school disentitle a student from pursuing studies just because he has kept a beard? Then there will be no end to such prima facie ridiculous rules."

This exemplifies the difficulties faced by the Court in dealing with two 'competing' constitutional rights in Articles 25 and 30. The first Bench obviously gave precedence to the group right guaranteed by the Constitution (Article 30) to a religious minority, in this case the Christian management of the school. The second Bench, on the other hand, deemed fit, in the context of the case, to uphold the right of the individual (Article 25), the Muslim boy.

This deep dilemma, as Justice Alam points out seems to run through the decisions of the Supreme Court on the issue of cultural and educational rights guaranteed by the Constitution to the religious minorities.

In 1957, the Communist Government of Kerala enacted a law bringing the school education in the State under its extensive control. A number of Christian organizations and some Muslim groups threatened to create a political crisis.

The President of India to whom the Bill had come for his assent therefore made a reference to the Supreme Court on the constitutional validity of the Bill. A Constitution Bench of seven Judges, headed by Chief Justice S.R. Das, heard the matter and held [AIR 1958 SC 956] that Article 30 was a *stand-alone* Article and the right guaranteed to the minorities under it was not controlled either by Article 29 or any other Article in the chapter of fundamental rights, or even Article 45 in the chapter of Directive Principles relating to education to children below the age of six years. Speaking for the Court S.R. Das, C.J. said:

"... So long as the Constitution stands as it is and is not altered, it is, we conceive, the duty of this Court to uphold the fundamental rights and thereby honour our sacred obligation to the minority communities who are our own" (p.986).

The decision in *Kerala Education Bill, 1957,* however, was not unanimous. There was at least one dissenting voice (of Justice

T.L. Venkatarama Aiyar.). He took the view that Article 30 was primarily intended to protect educational institutions established for the conservation and promotion of the *culture, language or religion* of a minority group and thus created a purely negative obligation on the State and prevented it from interfering with minorities living their own cultural life as regards religion or language.

Justice Aiyar observed:

"... Now, to compel the State to recognise those institutions would conflict with the fundamental concept on which the Constitution is framed *that the State should be secular in character*." (p.989)

The two views directly opposing each other and both relying upon the principles of secularism that were manifested in *Kerala Education Bill* appear to run through the decisions of the Supreme Court on all aspects of secularism.

But with the sole exception in *S. Azeez Basha* v. *Union of India(Aligarh Muslim University case* [AIR 1968 SC 662]) the majority decision in *Kerala Education Bill* was relied upon to expand the scope of the right under Article 30, and five years later in *Sidhrajbhai Sabbai* v. *State of Gujarat* (AIR 1963 SC 540) a six-Judge constitutional Bench went on to hold:

"The right [under] Article 30(1) is a fundamental right declared in terms absolute. Unlike the fundamental freedoms guaranteed by Article 19 *it is not subject to reasonable restrictions.*" (p.547).

Soon secularism came to be regarded as not only a fundamental right but a part of the basic structure of the Constitution. In the Bommai case [(1994)3 SCC 1] seven out of the nine Judges constituting the Bench reiterated the view that secularism was the basic feature of the Constitution and in case a State Government acted contrary to the constitutional mandate of secularism or, worse still, directly or indirectly, subverted the secular principles, *that would tantamount to failure of the constitutional machinery and the State Government would make itself liable to dismissal under Article 356* (para 434).

But soon enough, the Court started to see the interplay between the community-based rights and individual rights in a new light.

In *Stephen's College,* a Delhi Christian minority college the Court felt the need to strike a balance between an individual's right based on merits and the right of minorities to set up and administer educational institutions of their choice and directed that *St. Stephen's College* could have no more than fifty per cent seats reserved for Christian students.

Thus, the right under Article 30 was for the first time subject to Article 29 reversing the earlier ominous trend, for the better. Article 29 states:

Protection of interests of minorities.—(1) Any section of the citizens residing in the territory of India or any part thereof having a distinct language, script or culture of its own shall have the right to conserve the same.

As Justice Alam infers, by 2005, this reversing trend was fortified by several decisions till in the end of Article 30 all but lost its independent identity. The position that emerges from these decisions may be summarised thus:

- The right to set up educational institutions and impart any kind of education at any level is available to every Indian citizen under Article 19(1)(g) of the Constitution as the right "to carry on any occupation, trade or business."
- Article 30 does not give to the religious minorities any additional or separate right. *The religious minority has no*

special right that the majority does not have under the Constitution.

- Articles 29 and 30 do not confer any rights but afford certain protections to the minorities. The two articles can be better understood as a protection and/or a privilege of the minority rather than an abstract right. (View of Venkatarama, J. in minority of 1:6 in *Kerala Education Bill*, was thus resurrected!)
- The right under Article 30 is not absolute. It is subject to Article 29(2) and other laws. *It can be restricted in public interest and national interest.*

The Supreme Court's perception of secularism, also underwent change since the Bommai case of 1994 through a catena of judgments since 1995.

In 2002, a public interest litigation [(2002) 7 SCC368] was filed questioning the curriculum for school education framed by the National Council for Educational Research and Training on the ground that it was heavily loaded with religion and the contents of the Vedas.

It was contended that the inclusion of religion, Sanskrit, Vedic Mathematics, Vedic Astrology, etc. in the courses of study for the schools was contrary to secular principles.

Justice Dharmadhikari one of the members of the three-Judge Bench wrote a separate, though concurring judgment in which he discussed in some detail about the true nature of secularism.

He observed that the doctrine of the State neutrality towards all religions was a narrow concept of secularism. He further observed that the policy of complete neutrality towards and apathy for all kinds of religious teachings in institutions of the State had not done any good to the country.

The real meaning of secularism is 'sarva dharma samabhav' meaning equal treatment and respect for all religions, but, we misunderstood the meaning of secularism as negation of all religions." (page 406-407)

In 2005, an organisation representing a section of the Jain community came to the Court seeking a direction to the Central Government to notify "Jains" as a minority community.

The Court not only firmly rejected the prayer but also expressed its strong disapproval of the very concept of "minority." Calling it a baggage from India's history, the Court noted (*Bal Patil case, SCC* p. 701, para 25): "Muslims constituted the largest religious minority because the Mughal period of rule was the longest followed by the British Rule during which many Indians had adopted Muslim and Christian religions."

It further observed that the concept of "minorities" was the result of the British policy of divide and rule that first led to the formation of separate electorates and reservations of seats on the basis of population of Hindus and Muslims and finally led to the partition of India and formation of a separate Muslim State of Pakistan.

The Court pointed out that India was a democratic republic which had adopted the right to equality as its fundamental creed and hence, the constitutional ideal should be the elimination of "minority" and "majority" and the so-called forward and backward classes.

All that remains now is further decisions of the Supreme Court to restrict the meaning of minorities to cover *only ethnic minorities whose DNA is different from majority of Indians*. That would mean only a few tribes of extreme Northeast and Onge tribes in Andamans, but not Muslims and Christians who are not recent converts.

Affirmative action of the State however can be extended only to those minorities which have suffered from imposed disabilities, and not those minorities which have been ruling classes.

The term 'Secularism' should also be replaced in the Constitution by the alternative more appropriate phrase: "spiritual state," based on 'Sarva Pantha Sama Bhava'.

India today leads the world in the supply pool of youth, i.e., persons in the age group of 15 to 35 years, and this lead will last for another forty years.

This generation is most fertile milieu for promoting knowledge, innovation, and research. It is the prime work force that saves for the future, the corpus for pension funding of the old. We should therefore not squander this "natural vital resource."

Modern economic growth also is powered overwhelming (over 65% of GDP) by new innovation and techniques (e.g., internet). More capital and labour contributes less than 35% of growth in GDP.

We must hence by proper policy for the young, realize and harvest the demographic potential. China is the second largest world leader in young population today. But the youth population in that country will start shrinking from 2015, i.e., less than a decade from now because of lagged effect of their ill-thought one-child policy.

Japanese and European total populations are fast aging, and will start declining in *absolute* numbers from next year. The US will however hold a steady trend thanks to a liberal policy of immigration, especially from Mexico and Phillipines.

But even then the US will have in a decade hence a demographic shortage in skilled personnel. All currently developed countries thus experience a demographic deficit. *India will not.* Our past alleged liability, by a fortuitous turn of fate, has (now become to be globally regarded as our potential asset.

The primary object of education thus was for preparing the mind in all its facets. This training of the mind and the process of thinking were considered as pre-requisites essential for the acquisition of knowledge. Today, the West has re-invented this concept in the development of the intelligence in five dimensions-cognitive, emotional, social, moral and spiritual intelligences.

Thus, India has now become, by unintended consequences, gifted with a young population. If we educate this youth to develop and attain a high quotient of *cognitive intelligence* [CQ] to become original thinkers, imbibe *emotional intelligence* quotient [EQ] to have team spirit and rational risk-taking attitude, inculcate *moral intelligence* [MQ] to blend personal ambition with national goals, cultivate *social intelligence* [SoQ] to defend civic rights of the weak, gender equality, and the courage to fight injustice, nurture *spiritual intelligence* [SQ], *environmental intelligence* [EnQ], and *Innovational Intelligence* [InQ] to innovate the transformative power of vision and intention to access the vast energy the pervades the cosmos to innovate and out of box research, then we can develop a superior species of human being, a modern Indian youth who can be relied on to contribute to make India a global power within two decades.

Computers may have high CQ because they are programmed to understand the rules, and follow them without making mistakes.

Many mammals have high EQ. Only humans know to ask why, and can work with re-shaping boundaries instead of just within boundaries. Human can innovate, not animals.

The nation must therefore structure a national policy for the youth of India so that in every young Indian the seven dimensional concept of intelligence manifests in his character. Only then, our demographic dividend will not be wasted.

These seven dimensions of intelligence *constitute the ability of a person* to live a productive life and for national good. Hence, a policy for India's youth has to be structured within the implied parameters of these seven dimensions. What is, hence, essential is the character and integrity of its citizens. Thus, besides the objective of acquiring knowledge and getting employment that requires cognitive intelligence, the youth must be motivated imbibe in the other dimensions of intelligence in his outlook.

These concepts have been developed in the eighteen chapters of Bhagavat Gita, that have been interpreted in modern context by Sri Chandrashekharendra Sarasvati of Kanchi Mutt, Swami Chinmayananda, and Swami Dayananda Sarasvati of Arsha Vidyalaya.

In the United States, as the *Business Week* magazine reported [in 2006], these concepts have become highly popular in the corporate world, and which have also been incorporated in the best-selling books written by Daniel Goleman, Deepak Chopra, and Anthony Robbins among others.

In brief, the National Youth Policy is defined by measures by which we can create a modern mindset in the youth of India, not only to motivate the youth to acquire techrucal competence, but to develop values that will make that person a self-reliant individual of high character, patriotic, and possessing a social conscience.

Such an army of evolved youth will be the asset of the nation, and then collectively the demographic dividend can be reaped by us to usher National Renaissance for the glory of

Bharat Mata. A well structured national youth policy is vital for making India global power two decades hence which should also be our objective and a basis.

The majority-minority question has dogged India for the last seven decades and more years since Independence. Paradoxically, the Hindus despite being over 80% appear to suffer from a minority complex, because Hindus of today are being confused by others on whether the Republic of India founded in 1947 is a legatee of the ancient Hindu India, *or a new nation* altogether, forged as a by-product of British rule from a motley crowd of castes, ethnicities, and linguistic groups.

This confusion is also at the core of the identity crisis which can disappear if we decide which of these two we are: a continuing Hindu civilisational entity or an administrative by-product of British Imperialism.

Minorities would in turn need to understand how to adjust with the Hindu majority and to its own sub-legacy of forced or induced conversions to Islam and Christianity by foreign invaders, and thus whereby this identity crisis is resolved.

The present dysfunctional perceptional mismatch in the understanding of who are we as a people, is behind most of the communal tensions and inter-community distrust in the country. It also weakens India's integrity.

Unless Indians settle this question arising from these two conflicting concepts of identity clearly, finally, unambiguously, and authoritatively as to who we Indians are, Indians will flounder, flip-flop, and generally continue be devoid of healthy patriotism. That is we are Hindustanis of the soil of Bharat Mata.

CHAPTER 3

Defalsified Hindu History

The facts of our history have to be well understood so that we are not condemned to re-live it. Our national identity has been deliberately distorted by a history written about us by invading aggressors.

We have defined the Indian nation as "a nation of Hindus and those others who proudly acknowledge that their ancestors were Hindus."

But what the current history textbooks today teach is still basically the theory of a few nineteenth-century European "scholars" (including the paid agent of the East India Company viz., Max Muller).

According to them, around 1500 BC hordes of semi-barbarian, pastoral nomads, the so-called "Aryans," poured out of Europe/Central Asia into Northwest India, and drove south the ancestors of today's "Dravidians," then over a few centuries, they composed the Vedas, gradually got their "Aryan" culture (with its language, Sanskrit) to spread all over India, and eventually built the mighty Ganges civilization.

This is so estimated because the Hindus valley layers so far excavated in the Mohenjodaro/Harappa ruins, show destruction from unnatural causes of a city civilization, to be around 1500 BC, while the Rg Veda talks of a pastoral society. Thus pasting together, it means Vedic people destroyed the Indus Valley civilization.

This, with some variations, is still today what the school-going child is taught. Not only textbooks, even respectable dictionaries and encyclopaedias will tell you more or less the same thing.

However, today with new evidence tumbling out a debate rages not only in India but in Western universities and among eminent scholars and archaeologists. Many of them have in recent years called for a new look at this Aryan Invasion Theory (AIT).

All of them agree that archaeological evidence entirely fails to support the Aryan invasion theory and actually goes against it; many of them also find the linguistic evidence that was used to buttress it, quite shaky. But this debate, as we shall see, is by no means limited to the academic world; it is not a dry scholarly matter, and it has far-reaching repercussions on today's India, especially where her unity and Identity is concerned.

Such a "history" had been deliberately created by the British as a policy. Sir George Hamilton, Secretary of State for India, wrote on 26 March 1888 that "I think the real danger to our rule is not now but say 50 years hence.... We shall (therefore) break Indians into two sections holding widely different views.... We should so plan the educational text books that the differences between community and community are further strengthened."

After achieving independence, under the leadership of the Europeanised Jawaharlal Nehru and the implementing authority of the British set up ICS, revision of our history was never done. In fact the very idea was condemned as "obscurantist" and Hindu chauvinist.

The fabrication and falsification of our History begins with ancient India's chronology. The customary dates quoted for composition of the *Rig Veda* are: circa 1300 B.C., Mahabharat: 600 B.C., Buddha's *Nirvana:* 483 B.C., Maurya Chandragupta's coronation 324 B.C., and Ashoka: 268 B.C., These dates are entirely wrong.

Those dates are directly or indirectly based on a selected reading of Megasthenes' account of India: 'Indika'. In fact, so much so that eminent British trained historians have called Indika the "sheet anchor of Indian chronology."

The account of Megasthenes has also an important bearing on distant questions such as the two-race (Aryan-Dravidian) theory, and on the pre-Vedic character of the so-called Indus Valley Civilization.

Megasthenes was the Greek ambassador sent by Seleucus Nicator in c.302 B.C. to the court of the Indian king whom he and the Greeks called "Sandrocottus" stationed in "Palimbothra," the capital city of the kingdom.

His son was called Sandrocruptus by Megasthanes. It is not clear how many years Megasthenes stayed in India, but he did write an account of his stay, titled *Indika.*

The manuscript *Indika* is lost, and there is no copy of it available. However, during the time it was available, many other Greek writers quoted passages from it in their own works.

These quotations were meticulously collected by Dr. Schwanbeck in the nineteenth century, and the compilation is also available to us in English (J.M. McCrindle: *Ancient India as Described by Megasthenes and Arrian*).

When European indologists were groping clueless to date Indian history during the nineteenth century (after having arbitrarily rejected the various *Puranas),* the Megasthenes account came in very useful.

These scholars simply identified "Sandrocottus" with Chandragupta, and "Palimbothra" with Pataliputra. Since

Megasthenes talks of Sandrocottus as being a man not of "noble" birth who essentially usurped the throne from Xandrames and founded a new dynasty, the western writers took it as enough evidence to suggest that Sandrocottus was Chandragupta, who deposed the Nanda (=Xandrames) dynasty, and founded the Maurya dynasty. This identification, thus places Maurya Chandragupta circa 302 B.C.

However, Megasthenes also notes that Sandrocottus was a contemporary of Alexander, and came to the throne soon after Alexander's departure. With a little arithmetic on how many days it would have taken Alexander to cross the Indus, etc., the scholars arrive at c.324 B.C. as the date of Chadragupta Maurya's coronation.

It is on this date that every other date of Indian history has been founded and re-constructed. The western writers constructed other dates of Indian history by using the date on the number of years between kings given in the *Puranas,* even though they have generally discredited the Puranas.

For instance, the Puranas give the number of years for the reign of Chandragupta and Bindusara as 62 years. Using this period, Asoka's coronation year is calculated by them as 324-62=circa 262 B.C.

This estimated year is then cross-checked and adjusted with other indicators, such as from the Ceylonese Pali tradition. The point that is being made here is that some of the important dates of Indian history have been directly determined by the identification of Megasthenes' Sandrocottus with Maurya Chandragupta, and Xandremes with Nanda.

The founder of the Mauryas, however, *is not the only Chandragupta in Indian history*, who was a king of Magadh and founder of a dynasty. In particular, there is Gupta

Chandragupta, a Magadh king and founder of the Gupta dynasty at Pataliputra. Chandragupta Gupta was also not of "noble" birth and, in fact, came to power by deposing the Andhra king Chandrasri.

That is, Megasthenes', Sandrocottus may well be Gupta Chandragupta instead of Maurya Chandragupta (and Xandremes the same as Chandrasri, and Sandrocryptus as Samudragupta). In order to determine which Chandragupta it is, we need to look further.

It is, of course, a trifle silly to build one's history on this kind of tongue-gymnastics, but I am afraid we have no choice but to pursue the Megasthenes evidence to its end, since the currently acceptable but falsified history is based on it.

In order to determine at which Chandragupta's court Megasthenes was ambassador, we have to look further into his account of India. We find he was at Pataliputra. We know from the *Puranas* (which are unanimous on this point) that all the Chandravamsa king of Magadh (including the Mauryas) prior to the Guptas, had their capital at Girivraja (or equivalently Rajgrha) and not at Pataliputra.

Gupta Chandragupta was the first king to have his capital in Pataliputra. This alone should identify Sandrocottos with Gupta Chandragupta. However, this point is a bit controversial because some 11th century A.D. sources call Pataliputra the Maurya capital, e.g., Vishakdatta in *Mudrarakshasa*.

Pursuing Megasthenes' account further, we find most of it impossible to believe. He appears to be quite vague about details and is obviously given to the ancient Greek writers' weakness in letting his imagination get out of control.

For example, "Near a mountain which is called Nulo there live men whose feet are turned backwards and have eight toes on each foot." [See *Solinus* 52.36-30 XXX.B]: "Megasthenes says a race of men (exist in India) who neither eat or drink, and in fact have not even mouths, set on fire and burn like incense in order to sustain their existence with odorous fumes...." (Plutarch, Frag. XXXI).

However, Megasthenes appears to have made one precise statement of possible application which was picked up later by Pliny, Solinus, and Arrian. As summarized by Professor K.D. Sethna of Pondicherry, it reads:

"Dionysus was the first who invaded India and was the first of all who triumphed over the vanquished Indians. From the days of Dionysus to Alexander the Great, 6451 years reckoned with 3 months additional."

While there are a number of issues raised by this statement, the exactness with which he states his numbers should lead us to believe that Megasthenes could have received his chronological data from none else than the Puranic pundits of his time. To be conclusive, we need to determine who are the "Dionysus" of Megasthenes' account.

Traditionally, Dionysus (or Father Bachhus) was a Greek God of wine who was created from Zeus's thigh. Dionysus was also a great king, and was recognised as the first among all kings, a conqueror and constructive leader. There is a possible and credible Indian equivalent of Dionysus whom Megasthenes quickly equated with his God of wine. Looking through the Puranas, one does indeed find such a person. His name is Prithu.

Prithu was the son of King Vena. The latter was considered a wicked man whom the great sages could not tolerate, especially after he told them that the elixir *soma* should offered to him in prayer and not to the gods (*Bhagavata Purana* IV.14.28).

The great sages thereafter performed certain rites and killed Vena. But since this led immediately to lawlessness and chaos, the *rshis* decided to rectify it by coronating a strong and honest person. The *rshis* therefore churned the right arm (or thigh; descriptions vary) of the dead body (of Vena) to give birth to a fully grown Prithu.

It was Prithu, under counsel from *rshi* Atri (father of *Soma)*, who reconstructed society and brought about economic prosperity. Since he became such a great ruler, the *Puranas* have called him *adi-raja* (first king) of the world. So did the Satapatha Brahmana (v.3.5 4.).

In the absence of a cult of *Soma* in India, it is perhaps inevitable that Megasthenes and the other Greeks, in translating Indian experiences for Greek audiences, should pick on adi-raja Prithu who is "tinged with Soma" in a number of ways and bears such a close resemblance to Dionysus in the circumstances of his birth, and identify him as Dionysus.

If we accept identifying Dionysus with Prithu, then indeed by a calculation based on the *Puranas* (done by D.R. Mankad, Koti Venkatachelam, K.D. Sethna, and others), it can be conclusively shown that indeed 6451 years had elapsed between Prithu and a famous Chandragupta.

This calculation exactly identifies Sandrocottus with Gupta Chandragupta and not with Maurya Chandragupta.

This calculation must be necessarily long and tedious to counter the uninformed general feeling first sponsored by Western scholars, that the *Puranas* spin only fairy tales and are therefore quite unreliable. However, most of these people do not realize that most *Puranas* have six parts, and the *Vamsanucharita* sections (especially of Vishnu, Matsya, and Vagu) are a systematic presentation of Indian history especially of the Chandravamsa kings of Magadha.

In order to establish these dates, I would have to discuss in detail the cycle of lunar asterisms, the concept of them according to Aryabhatta, and various other systems, and also the reconciliation of various minor discrepancies that occur in the *Puranas*. Constraints of space, however, prevent me from presenting these calculations here.

On the basis of these calculations we can say that Gupta Chandragupta was "Sandrocottus" c.327 B.C. His son, Samudragupta, was the great king who established a unified kingdom all over India, and obtained from the Cholas, Pandyas, and Cheras their recognition of him.

Samudragupta also gave a beating of Seleucus Nicator, while his father Chandragupta was king. On this calculation we can also place Prithu at 6777 B.C.. Derivation of other dates without discussion may also be briefly mentioned: Buddha's Nirvana 1807 B.C., Maurya Chandragupta c. 1534 B.C., Harsha Vikramaditya (Parmar) c. 82 B.C.

Arun Bansal, who pioneered computer casting of horoscopes has, using astronomical data on planet positions given in the Puranas, determined that Lord Krishna was born on 21 July 3228 B.C and went back to his heavenly abode on 18 February 3102, when Kaliyug started. Western scholars accept the Puranic sequence of dynasty and Kings, so why not the dates?

Instead Western scholars have constructed an enormous edifice of dates to suit their contrived chronology of Indian history.

A number of them are based on misidentification. For instance, the Rock Edict XIII, the famous Kalinga edict, is identified as Asoka's. It was, however, Samudragupta's.

Samudragupta was a great conqueror and a devout admirer of Asoka. He imitated Asoka in many ways and also took the name Asokaditya. In his later life he too became a sanyasi or monk.

The Ceylonese Pali traditions leave out the Cholas, Pandyas, and Cheras from the list of Asoka's kingdoms, whereas Rock Edict XIII includes them. In fact, as many scholars have noted, the character of Asoka from Ceylonese and other traditions is precisely (as R.K. Mukherjee has said) what does not appear in the principal edicts.

Facts which directly contradict Westerners theories, they have rather flippantly cast aside. We state here only two examples of such facts: (1) Fa-hsien was in India and at Pataliputra c.410 A.D. He mentions a number of kings, but makes not even a fleeting reference to the Gupta Kingdom, even though according to European scholars he came during the height of their reign. He also dates Buddha at 1100 B.C. (2) A number of Tibetan documents place Buddha at 2100 B.C..

Thus, when we examine the accounts of ancient India as given in current history books still in use against the background of available data and the primary sources, we find a fundamental mismatch between scientific evidence and facts and historical theories propounded. As number of Indian scholars and institutions have begun to challenge the West-tutored falsified history.

For example, Dr. N.S. Rajaram has admirably summarized this in his works debunking the bogus Aryan-Dravidian divide:

1. There is no Indian archaeological record of any invasion and/or massive migration from Eurasia in the Vedic period. If anything we find traces of movement in the opposite direction—to West Asia and even Europe.

2. The geography described in the *Rigveda* corresponds to North India in the fourth millennium BC and earlier and not Europe or Eurasia.

3. The flora and fauna described in the Vedic literature, especially those found in the sacred symbols, are tropical and

subtropical varieties and not from the temperate climate or the steppes.

4. The climate corresponds to that found in North India.

The Aryan-Dravidian divide in the history taught in schools and universities is purely a conception of foreign historians like Max Mueller and has no basis in India historical records. This fraudulent history has been lapped up by many upper caste Indians, as their racial passport to Europe.

Such has been the demoralization of the Hindu mind, which we have to shake off through a new factual account of our past History.

But today, the bogus British imposed theory is being challenged by two new discoveries, one archaeological and the other linguistic. Firstly, in the Rig Veda, the Ganges, India's sacred river, is only mentioned once, but the mythic Saraswati is praised fifty times.

For a long time, the Saraswati river was indeed considered a myth, until the American satellite Landstat was able to photograph and map the bed of this magnificent river, which was nearly 14 km wide and took its source in the Himalayas.

Archaeologist Paul-Henri Francfort, who studied the Saraswati region at the beginning of the Nineties, found out the Saraswati had "disappeared," because around 2200 B.C., an immense drought reduced the whole region to aridity and famine. "Thus," he writes, "most inhabitants moved away from the Saraswati to settle on the banks of the Indus and Sutlej rivers."

As the discovery of the Saraswati river, the decipherment of the Indus scripts also goes to prove that the Harappan civilization, of which the seals are a product, belonged to the latter part of the Vedic Age and had close connections with Vedantic works like the Sutras and the Upanishads.

Hence, it is becoming more and more clear that there never was an Aryan invasion in India, a theory which was imposed upon the subcontinent by its colonisers and is today kept alive by Nehruvian historians such as Romila Thapar missionaries (to convert the drowntrodden tribals and Dravidians, by telling them that Hinduism was a religion thrust upon them by the hated "Brahmin" invaders) and the Communists (who hate anything Hindu).

But as long as India will not rewrite its history books and teach its children to be proud of its ancient and indigenous civilization, there will be others who will come and exploit India.

Using the astronomy techniques following pivotal events of the Lord Ramayana at the following point in time:

Lord Rama's birth : 4 December 7323 B.C.,

Lord Rama's marriage with Sita : 7 April 7307 B.C.,

Lord Rama's exile : 29 November 7306 B.C.,

Hanuman's entry to Lanka : 1 September 7292 B.C.,

Construction of Setu (bridge) : 26-30 Oct. 7292 B.C.,

The beginning of the great war : 3 November 7292 B.C.

Ravana's killing by Lord Rama : 15 November 7292 B.C.

Lord Rama's return to Ayodhya : 16 November 7292 B.C.

As Dr. N.S. Rajaram has noted we now have the technical tools needed to unlock the secrets of our past, but it needs dedicated study and research in several disciplines. It is important, however, to familiarize oneself with the basics of human genetics to be able to make use of the wealth of ideas and data that are becoming available to historians.

This calls for a new generation of historians that is more educated in science, as also less deferential towards anything handed down by Western academia. Humanities scholars in

India need to catch up with the confidence developed by Indian scientists and technologists.

Sri Aurobindo wrote seven decades ago that "Indian scholars have not been able to form themselves into a great and independent school of learning is due to two causes: the miserable scantiness of the mastery in Sanskrit provided by our universities, crippling to all but born scholars, and our lack of sturdy independence which makes us over-ready to defer to European [and Western] authority." How true it is even today!

Thus the history of no free country can be structured on foreign accounts of it. The time has come for us to take seriously our Puranic sources and to imbibe a de-falsified and well-founded history of ancient India, a history written by Indians about Indians.

Such a re-written history would bring out the amazing continuity of a nation, which nation asserted its identity again and again at times of war and political crises.

It should focus on the fact that at the centre of our perception of Indian nation is the concept of the *Chakravartin* ideal—to defend the nation from external aggression while giving maximum internal autonomy to the *janapadas*.

A correct, defalsified history would record that Hindustan was conceptually one in the art of governance, in the style of royal courts, in the methods of warfare, in the maintenance of its agrarian base, and in the dissemination of information. Otherwise it was decentralized for autonomy of villages in self-administration. The Panchayat system is a manifestation of that.

The correct perception of Indian identity is we are a people who have always constituted a nation living in a geographical location spanning from Kashmir to Kanyakumari, from Attak to Car Nicobar, bound together in a continuing civilization of more than 10,000 years, a people who are mostly of Hindu religious faith or of those others of separate but equally respected faith, whose ancestry is however Hindu.

A rudderless India so far, disconnected from her past has, as a consequence, become a fertile field for religious poachers and neo-imperialists from abroad who paint India as a mosaic of immigrants much like a crowd on a platform in a railway junction.

That is, it is clandestinely propagated that India has belonged to those who forcibly occupied it and gave it an identity. This is the theme around which the Islamic fundamentalists and fraud Christian crusaders are again at work, much as they were a thousand years ago, but of course in new dispensations, sophistication, and media forms.

The Hindu unity of India has to be seen from time immemorial. Sri Aurobindo never tired of stressing this essential unity:

"In India," he said, "at a very early time the spiritual and cultural unity was made complete and became the very stuff of the life of all this great surge of humanity between the Himalayas and the two seas.

Sri Aurobindo also said:

"A time must come when the Indian mind will shake off the darkness that has fallen upon it, cease to think or hold opinions at second and third hand and reassert its right to judge and enquire in a perfect freedom into the meaning of its own Scriptures. When that day comes we shall, I think, {.....} question many established philological myths – the legend, for instance, of an Aryan invasion of India from the north, the artificial and inimical distinction of Aryan and Dravidian which an erroneous philosophy has driven like a wedge into the unity of the homogenous Indo-afghan race."

This intrinsic Hindu unity has thus been sought during the last two centuries to be undone by legitimizing such bogus concepts as Aryan-Dravidian racial divide theory, or that India as a concept never existed till the British imperialists invented it, or that Indians have always been ruled by invaders from abroad.

Thus the concept of intrinsic Hindu unity, and India's Hindu foundation are thus dangerously under challenge by these forces. Tragically most Hindus today are not even cognizant of it. Thomas Babington Macaulay who vowed that by change in India's educational system he would create a class of Indians in blood and colour, but English in taste, in opinions, in morals, and intellect, has eminently succeeded. The Hindutva movement based on Vedantic principles must undo this erroneous and dysfunctional assimilation.

Another deliberate misrepresentation of Indian history by the British was of the First War of Independence which the British re-named disparagingly as "Indian Mutiny."

On 10 May 1857, Indian soldiers of the regiments stationed at Meerut (U.P.) killed their British officers, marched to Delhi and liberated the city from British control.

They then proclaimed the 82 year old Bahadur Shah Zafar as the "Emperor of Hindustan." The Emperor then appointed a Hindu as his 'Prime Minister' Mukund Ram just as Nana Saheb Baji Rao, the adopted son of the Peshawas and partner in the revolt, appointed a Muslim, Azimullah as his 'Prime Minister'. At Red Fort, the Bhagwa Dhwaj (saffron flag) was unfurled.

The uprising did not last long. In Delhi it was over by September 1857, and the domino effect in the country as a whole of the revolt was contained by end 1858. But the popular uprising fired the imagination of the nation and from the ashes of the burnt out revolution, sparks continued to ignite revolt in the country till Mahatma Gandhi led the nation finally to Freedom in 1947.

Exactly 160 years later today, however, the whole of India has become oblivious of this historic date and of the event that was the foreunner of India's freedom.

No meetings, no TV discussions, no resolutions for this revolutionary day in a country which is ready to celebrate or mourn anything or anybody. During the UPA reign, even for a Pope in far away Vatican we mourned for three days when the rest of the world except Italy did not see it fit to do so.

We forgot 10 May 1857 because we were programmed since then for nearly a century to delete it from out collective memory. After achieving Independence in 1947, the amnesia was not cured by Free India's government.

The British imperialists who understood the significance and import of the 1857 uprising, had ensured that it be ridiculed and downgraded as a "Sepoy mutiny," as a sporadic and limited uprising of soldiers that was ignited due to obscurantist reasons such as aversion to 'pig fat' in the cartridges. Not only the Imperialists, but the Marxist thinkers as well sought to play it down as a 'reaction'.

Writing in New York Daily Tribune in a series of articles in 1857, Karl Marx termed it as an army revolt, "a military mutiny" but of national proportion only because "the natives' apprehension" that Government may otherwise interfere with their religion.

It was much later in 1957 a hundred year later that Marxist writer P.C. Joshi corrected the perspective of the party line. Others like Sir John Kaye, a prolific scribe, wrote that 1857 was due to the "fear on part of the Brahmins of the social changes" introduced by the British !!

It was Veer Savarkar however who in 1909 challenged this diminution and degradation of the 1857 uprising. He wrote his account of 1857 under the title "The Indian War of Independence: 1857." It was printed in Holland, but nevertheless the British authorities proscribed it.

Savarkar re-interpreted 1857 as a war of independence, and his magnum opus served to fire the imagination of the youth for years to come till 1947.

Savarkar's contribution to nation building by his well researched and scientific analysis of 1857 uprising the First War of Independence shall remain everlasting and deserving of a Bharat Ratna.

Only those brain washed by the British Imperialist can devalue it or detract from its seminal character. Savarkar saw the 1857 uprising as a national spirit that aroused "sepoy and civilian, king and pauper, Hindu and Mahomedan" to a revolution.

In his book the Indian War of Independence of 1857, he asks:

"What, then were the real causes and motives of this revolution? What were they that for them men by the thousand willingly poured their blood year after year? What were they that Maulvis preached them, learned Brahmins blessed them that for their success prayers went up to Heaven from the mosques of Delhi and the temples of Benares?" And he answered this question as "These great principles were Swadharma (one's duty) and Swaraj {self-government}."

Savarkar approvingly quotes the newly installed 'Emperor of Hindustan's Proclamation' as stating:

"Hindus and Mohamedans of India! Arise! Brethern arise! Of all the gifts of God, the most gracious is that of Swaraj. God does not wish that you should remain idle. He has inspired in the hearts of Hindus and Mohamedans the desire to turn the English out of our country."

Thus Savarkar credits Nana Sahib, Bahadur Shah Zafar, Rani of Jhansi, and Khan Bahadur Khan of Rohilkhand along with the priests (Brahmins and Maulvis) of forcefully attempting a national consciousness of Hindustan to liberate the nation from foreigners.

The Hindustan, a term used by both Hindus and Muslims even today to describe India, would be 'Swadesh' for both Hindus and Muslims. Savarkar explains this adherence to the concept of Hindustan as follows:

"As long as the Mohamedans lived in India in the capacity of rulers, so long, to be willing to live with like brothers was to acknowledge national weakness. Hence, it was up to then, necessary to consider the Mahomedans as foreigners." And naturally so since no Muslim ruler adopted a secular state, and in fact adopted discriminatory taxes based on religion. Conversion to Islam was carried out by force, coercion and cruelty as evidenced in the tribulation suffered by Guru Teg Bahadur. So where was the question of brotherhood?

Savarkar then holds that after the heroism of Guru Gobind, Rana Pratap and the Maharattas, that grievance was no more valid, and that the original distinction between the Hindus and Muslims "must be laid to eternal rest."

Both communities, he adds in his magnum opus, are children of the soil of Hindustan, children of the same Mother India and of the same blood. He exhorted all to "create a passionate desire in the Hindustan for this ideal, and make all the country to rise simultaneously for the purpose of achieving it."

The 1857 spirit and the magnificient articulation of it by Veer Savarkar stood us in good stead throughout the Freedom Struggle. It was ultimately dertailed and destroyed by one "Himalayan Blunder" and two acts of treachery. The blunder was the Khilafat Movement of Mahatma Gandhi which he himself acknowledged as his Himalayan Blunder.

By opposing the modernizing secular movement of Kamaal Ataturk in Turkey, Gandhi dignified reactionary conservative movement amongst Muslims of India, and rethroned the concepts of Darul Islam {Muslim ruled states} and Darul Harab {Muslims in violent rebellion in non Muslim ruled states} in large enough measure in the Muslim mind.

But it was the betrayal of Jawaharlal Nehru of the 1937 Lucknow electoral pact with Khaliq uz Zaman of the Muslim League that shocked the Muslims especially those Muslims who had wanted to be partners with Hindus in the Freedom Movement [by acknowledging that they were both children of Mother India seeking to liberate her].

Nehru wriggled out of a pre-election agreement with the Muslim League to share in power in the UP Government after finding that Congress party had won majority on its own. This betrayal of a written pact swung emotional Muslims to demand Pakistan for the first time in 1940 at the Lahore session of the Muslim League.

Nehru again in 1946 by addressing a provocative press conference in Bombay sabotaged all efforts by Gandhi to effect a transfer of power from the British without Partition. Pakistan became a certainty that day, and the Hindu-Muslim brotherhood which flowered from 1857 onwards was subverted and finally laid to rest in 1947.

But the framework for Hindu Muslim brotherhood that Savarkar so brilliantly set out in his The War of Independence

1857 can to be revived. At some later date after the menance of Pakistani terrorism is sorted out finally.

Till then we must celebrate 10 May 1857 as equal to, if not more than 15 August 1947. The threat from the Feringhi {foreigner} is today as real as in 1857 and the nation must unite for it, without any appeasement or compromise on the ancient roots of Hindustan.

CHAPTER 4

Sanskrit as National Link Language

In India's long continuous history, Sanskrit has been the greatest integrating force, the source of cultural continuum, the medium of literary creativity, the voice of the sages and the language of the most sublime thoughts and the profoundest of the philosophies of life.

It was the medium of intellectual and spiritual discourse and made its impact on scholars throughout the length and breadth of the country.

A Virat Hindu needs to learn Sanskrit to have this access to this vast ocean of knowledge.

In the centuries to come, it is Sanskrit that will be the most sensible link language for us Indians. There are two reasons for it. The first is that all Indian languages have a high proportion of words taken from Sanskrit. In the case of Bengali and Malayalam it may be 90 per cent, while in the case of Tamil it is at least 42 per cent (even in the DMK version of "pure" Tamil).

Bengali is proudly referred to as the "daughter" of Sanskrit, but Tamil which has a proud history of its own, thanks to the long unbroken reign of the Chola kingdoms, is accepted by Sanskrit scholars as the "sister" of Sanskrit.

For this reason, Sanskritized Hindi is easier to understand for the Southerners (and difficult for those Northerners like Nehru steeped in Urdu). The late Annadurai of DMK used to say that for Sanskritized Hindi, "naa vadiyar" (I am teacher).

Incidentally, the Tamil word "vadiyar" is a respectable way to address from the Sanskrit word "vadi" (preacher).

For this reason of common vocabulary, Sanskrit is ultimately the best national link language for India.

Secondly, international research in today's most advanced area of computers, namely, Artificial Intelligence, which is to revolutionize the knowledge systems of the 21st Century, is now increasingly coming to the conclusion that Sanskrit is the best language to store knowledge in a computer.

Dr. Rick Briggs of the US National Aeronautics and Space Agency (NASA), in an article [12] titled "Knowledge Representation in Sanskrit and Artificial Intelligence" that:

"In the past twenty years, much time, effort, money has been expended on designing an unambiguous representation of natural languages to make them accessible to computer processing. Understandably, there is widespread belief that natural languages are unsuitable for the transmission of many ideas that artificial languages can render with great precision and mathematical rigour. There is at least one language, Sanskrit ... (in which) can be reckoned a method ... that is identical not only in essence but in form with current work in Artificial Intelligence."

This article demonstrates that a natural language (Sanskrit) can serve as an artificial language also, and that much work in Artificial Intelligence has been reinventing a wheel millenia old."

The grammarian—Panini—is now being called the first software man, without the hardware. And the focus is on the roughly 4,000 rules of Sanskrit grammar that the evolved. Rules that are so scientific and logical in manner that they closely resemble structures used by computer scientists throughout the world.

Since Sanskrit is said to be the mother of most Indian languages [Tamil being a sister of Sanskrit], scientists are trying to develop a mathematical and computational grammar for them.

These are "catchy ideas" in artificial intelligence today, with pioneering work now being done in India, US and Germany. Interestingly, many scientists are tempted to speculate how Panini developed his rules in so concise and precise a manner without a computer in 3995 aphorisms in his *Ashtadhyayi*.

Thus, as we look back, it seems that the founding fathers of the Independence Movement committed a blunder in not according Sanskrit its rightful place. Sanskrit is an essential component of the substance of Indian Asmita.

What came out of all that discussion in the Constituent Assembly was that Sanskrit was included in the 8th Schedule of the Constitution as one of the Indian languages (the number of these languages has now gone up to 18).

Also, it was provided that Hindi, which was to the official language and written in Sanskrit's Devanagari script [Article 340 of the Constitution], would be developed by drawing wherever necessary for its vocabulary primarily on Sanskrit [Article 351]. This was a "holding operation" compromise for make it a link language.

Nehru himself continued to pretend reverence for Sanskrit. While speaking in Parliament on a Private Member's Bill in 1959, Nehru *inter alia* said that people grew from their roots. India had a history of 5,000 to 10,000 years. Language was a symbol of continuity. The language to which most Indian languages were connected was Sanskrit. But it was lip service. In reality Nehru sabotaged the cause of Sanskrit. He made fun of All India Radio Hindi broadcasts as being "incomprehensible" to him.

Sanskrit has made the most significant contribution to the development of all the Indian languages. With the exception of four languages of the South, almost all the major Indian languages had their source and derived their sustenance from Sanskrit. The languages of the South also had a large part of their vocabulary derived from Sanskrit.

Anti-Hindi zealots today confuse Devanagiri with Hindi. The truth is that Hindi is just one of the languages using this script of Sanskrit. Marathi, Sindhi, and some of the Hill tract languages also use Devanagiri. This script thus can be used by any language. In fact, the scripts of all Indian languages even including Tamil and *Devanagiri* [considered as "sisters"] are direct descendants of the original *Brahmi* script. Any competent linguist would tell you that.

The *Gurumukhi* script is very similar to the *Devanagiri* script, just as the Gujarati script is. Anyone who knows *Devanagiri* can master Gurumukhi in 24 hours. Yet a senseless agitation took place to oppose Gurumukhi in Punjab, followed by an unhealthy polarization process that culminated in Operation Bluestar in 1984, the tragic after-effects of which, we feel even today.

In a calm dispassionate atmosphere which may take decades to attain, young people, especially those entering primary and secondary schools, should be made to learn at least two languages and two scripts: (1) mother tongue and Sanskrit and (2) own script and Devanagiri.

In the meantime, Hindi should continue to Sanskritize itself to the point where it becomes almost indistinguishable from Sanskrit. It will then merge into Sanskrit, disappearing excepting in local dialects.

Sanskrit was once long ago uprooted from India by Pali. But

after some centuries, this versatile language was rethroned by the same process via *Mahayana* Buddhism and by Sanskritising the vocabulary of Pali.

A second rethroning of Sanskrit can now be achieved through Sanskritising Hindi. Till that day, the three languages formula, which requires northerners to learn one southern language, if sincerely implemented, we can make a steady progress towards the goal of re-throning Sanskrit once again the national link language of India.

CHAPTER 5

Integral Humanism

In 1969, I had presented a "Swadeshi Plan" at the Patna Session of the Bharatiya Jana Sangh. It was an instant national event. So much so, that Prime Minister Mrs Indira Gandhi, who then also held the Finance Portfolio, on 4 March 1970 took the floor of the Lok Sabha during the 1970-71 Budget debate to denounce the Swadeshi Plan, and in particular me by name, as "dangerous."

She was particularly irked by my thesis that if India gave up socialism for competitive market economic system, then India can grow at 10% per year, achieve self-reliance and produce nuclear weapons.

Those days in the 1970s, few dared to question socialism. The entire Left wing academia therefore pounced on me because I debunked the Soviet economic model by describing it as a prescription for disaster for India. I was however proved right and vindicated later in 1991, when as Commerce Minister, I presented the first blue prints for economic reform that was subsequently adopted by the Narasimha Rao government.

Hence, my Swadeshi Plan was noticed and discussed nationwide by intellectuals and the media following Mrs Gandhi's outburst. Her Education Minister Nurul Hasan, and a Soviet agent, on her, then ensured that I lost my professorship at IIT, Delhi in 1972 [to which post I was re-instated twenty years later by a Delhi Court].

The Swadeshi Plan was influenced by Deendayal Upadhyaya's Integral Humanism, and by Dattopant Thengadi's commentaries on it. Guru Golwalkar, the Sarsanghchalak of the RSS, had also spoken to me about the best suited economic policy for India. Guruji motivated me when in 1970 I met him after I had returned to India from a long tenure as professor of economics at Harvard University USA.

Guru Golwalker, the RSS Chief (1940-1973) had long foreseen the debilitating effects of materialist outlook on human society, and long before the consumerism of globalization that we see today. He advocated the harmonization of material pursuits with spiritual and moral values to create an integral person. Guruji himself told me in 1970 that "swadeshi [self-reliance] and vikendrikaran [decentralization] are the two concepts which can summarise the economic policy suitable for our times." He added that economic policy thus designed must be consistent with the spiritual values of our ancient nation. It is this embryonic idea that Deendayal Upadhyaya developed into his thesis of *Integral Humanism.* To quote Deendayalji himself:

"Both these systems, capitalist and communist, have failed to take account of the Integral Man, his true and complete personality, and his aspirations. One [system] considers him as mere selfish being, lingering after money, having only one law, the law of fierce competition, in essence the law of the jungle; whereas the other has viewed him as a feeble lifeless cog in the whole scheme of things regulated by rigid rules, and incapable of any good unless directed. The centralization of power, economic and political, is implied in both. Both therefore result in dehumanization of man" [*Integral Humanism,* Navchetan Press, Delhi, 1965, p.76].

Deendayaiji also dismissed democratic or 'Gandhian' Socialism as failing to establish the importance of the human being [op.cit., p.74-75]. He said: "The needs and preferences of individuals have as much importance in the socialist system as in a prison manual."

This is in keeping with Guruji's thoughts [Bunch of Thoughts, p. 13] that class struggle as a concept embedded in socialism, is anti-human, and instead, class harmony and conflict resolution are the basic instincts of the human. Guruji stated that the Communist concept of the dictatorship of the proletariat was nothing but "the dictatorship of the dictator of a dictatorial party."

Thus now well past the centennial year of Sri Guruji's birth, we can proudly assert that he gave the nation a new direction in economics by propounding the concept of integral outlook—namely that economic behaviour must blend with spiritual values to produce a happy society.

We in this country have yet to incorporate this direction in our economic policy, but time will soon be at hand for us to do so when the people's mandate is given for a new system of governance.

Subsequently when I became Secretary of the Deendayal Research Institute (1971-75), it became clear to me that Guruji's ideas had been incorporated by Deendayal Upadhyaya in his *Integral Humanism* and also by Dattopant Thengadi in his *Ekatma Manavad. Ek Adhyan* [Rashtra Dharma Pustak Prakashan Lucknow 1970] and in his "Bharatiya Conception of Economic Order" [published in *The Perspectives,* Sahitya Sindhu Publishers, Bangalore, 1971].

Dattopant Thengadi also summarized in point form the discourse he gave in a meet in Thane, Maharashtra in 1973 just before his demise. This was published in *Organizer* weekly and I am thankful to Dattreya Hosbale for retrieving it for me.

Recently, I also had a discussion with the former Sarsangh chalak of RSS, Sudarshan on what type of economic policy would suit our civilization and values. Sudarshanji gave me some valuable suggestions on the subject which I have incorporated here.

In 1977, at the invitation Dr. Mahesh Mehta, I presented a paper in New York titled "Economic Perspectives in Integral Humanism." This was later published in a volume [edited by Mahesh Mehta] titled: *Upadhyaya's Integral Humanism* (Edison, NJ, 1978). Based on these works and researches, I have written this Chapter.

I am *not* an advocate of the concept of "Hindu economics." Economic laws are universal, and humans respond to incentives and coercion more or less the same way everywhere and in every culture.

But I do advocate here that ancient Hindu spiritual values, codified as: *Sanatana Dharma* [i.e., eternally valid enlightened norms] informing the pursuit of *artha* (wealth), *kama* (sensual pleasures) and *moksha* (spiritual salvation)], which informs the choice of objectives, priorities, strategy and financial architecture should structure the nation's economic policy. True happiness is possible only if material progress is attained moderated and harmonized by spiritual values.

As Bruce Rich in his: *To Uphold the World: A Call for a New Global Ethic from Ancient India* [Beacon Press, Boston, MA, USA, 2010] has aptly summarized it [on page 6] quoting Kautilya, otherwise known as Chanakya, that sequentially subject to dharma, priority be given to artha, i.e., the society's and individual's material wealth and well-being, with the subsequent aim of experiencing kama but ultimately striving to attain moksha. These last two goals are dependent on attaining a critical level of artha, much as later in the late nineteenth century Swami Vivekananda said that we cannot preach spirituality to someone with an empty stomach.

This is the 'Swadeshi' [indigenous] or Hindutva [the quality of being Hindu or Hindu-ness] theory of development wherein the main goal in life is the spiritual advancement of one's self as the basis for inner happiness, with economic well-being as a means to that end, contrasted with the single-minded pursuit of material and physical pleasure as an end in itself in capitalistic or socialistic theories of development and which uni-dimensional approach of materialism guides the present greed dominating globalization.

In 1970, I had presented a "Swadeshi Plan" [see my *Indian Economic Planning—An Alternative Approach*, Vikas, New Delhi, 1971] at a gathering of economists assembled at the Institute of Economic Growth, University of Delhi. It was an instant national media event because of the yearning for an alternative theory relevant to India, but attracted a huge flak from the Left-wing academics who dominated the universities those days.

So much so, that the Left leaning Prime Minister, Mrs Indira Gandhi, who also held the Finance Portfolio that time, on 4 March 1970 took the floor of the Lok Sabha [India's Parliament] during the 1970-71 Budget debate, to denounce the Swadeshi Plan, and me by name, as "dangerous" and re named me "Santa Claus."

She was particularly irked by my thesis that if India gave up socialism for competitive market economic system—tinged with nationalistic Hindu values much as Gandhi had preached about indigenous values and trusteeship, then India could grow at 10% per year, achieve self-reliance and produce nuclear weapons for its defence.

Those days in the 1970s, few dared to question socialism much less advocate Hindutva. The entire Left wing academia therefore had pounced on me and ostracized me from academia because I debunked the Soviet economic model by describing it as a prescription for disaster for India.

I was however proved right and vindicated later in 1991, when as Commerce Minister, I presented the first blue prints for economic reform that was subsequently adopted and implemented without much opposition by the successor Narasimha Rao government [in which I held a Cabinet rank post]. By then the Soviet Union had unraveled in a spectacle of 'Balkanisation' of 16 separate countries. Most of the prominent Left academics also migrated to the US.

In the late Seventies, I came under the influence of Deendayal Upadhyaya's Integral Humanism, and by Dattopant Thengadi's commentaries on it, and therefore enlarged the concept of *Swadeshi*, to explicitly include the necessacity of formally harmonizing the goal of economic development with India's ancient Hindu spiritual values.

In 1977, at the invitation Dr. Mahesh Mehta, I presented a paper in New York titled "Economic Perspectives in Integral Humanism." This was later published in a volume [edited by Mahesh Mehta] titled: *Upadhyaya's Integral Humanism* (Edison, NJ, 1978).

By then I had also been influenced by the writings of the venerated sage, accomplished scholar, and Freedom Fighter, Sri Aurobindo who had long foreseen the debilitating effects of an one-dimensional materialist outlook on human society, and long before the consumerism of globalization that we see today.

In his 1918 publication titled *The Renaissance of India,* he advocated the harmonization of material pursuits with spiritual and moral values to create an integral person. The economic policy thus designed must be consistent with the spiritual values of embedded in *Sanatana Dharma*.

It is this seminal idea that Deendayal Upadhyaya, a profound political thinker and activist, developed into his thesis of *Integral Humanism.* To quote Deendayalji himself:

"Both the systems, capitalist and communist, have failed to take account of the Integral Man, his true and complete personality, and his aspirations. One [system] considers him as mere selfish being, lingering after money, having only one law, the law of fierce competition, in essence the law of the jungle; whereas the other has viewed him as a feeble lifeless cog in the whole scheme of things regulated by rigid rules, and incapable of any good unless directed. The centralization of power, economic and political, is implied in both. Both therefore result in dehumanization of man" [*Integral Humanism,* Navchetan Press, Delhi, 1965, p.76]. He thus advocated that "swadeshi [self-reliance] and vikendrikaran [decentralization] as the two pillars of the economic policy suitable for our times.

Upadhyaya also dismissed democratic or "Gandhian' version of Socialism as failing to establish the importance of the human being [op. cit., p.74-75]. He said: "The needs and preferences of individuals have as much importance in the socialist system as in a prison manual."

This is in keeping with the thesis of Sri Aurobindo that class struggle as a concept embedded in socialism, is anti-human, and instead, class harmony and conflict resolution are the basic instincts of the human. The Communist concept of the dictatorship of the proletariat was nothing but "the dictatorship of the dictator of a dictatorial party."

Today I can with some satisfaction assert that the Hindutva Theory of economic development represents for the nation a new and alternative direction in economics discourse by propounding the concept of an integral outlook—namely that economic behaviour must blend with spiritual values to produce a happy and contented society.

We in India have yet to incorporate this direction in our official economic policy, but time will soon be at hand for us to do so when the people's mandate is given for a new system of governance.

In analyzing Integral Humanism as economic policy we need to structure it in a four dimensional framework as follows: (i) Objectives (2) Priorities (3) Strategy (4) The Financial and Institutional Architecture.

Let us take the first dimension, of objectives of economic policy of four main ideologies of Capitalism, Socialism, Communism and Integral Humanism.

Theoretically, Communism takes maximum production for the state as the goal, while capitalism considers that the jungle concept of *laissez faire* based on survival of the fittest will be guided by an Invisible Hand to achieve maximum profit for producers and maximum consumption of material goods for the worker.

Socialism aims at maximum welfare measured by state guarantees against risks of disease, death and unemployment to the individual citizen. That is the concept of welfare under socialism.

However all these goals are purely materialistic and derails the innate human development by encouraging the rat-race. Integral Humanism on the other hand requires the human being's development being viewed *integrally* and *holistically* (hence Upadhyaya's term 'Integral Humanism').

That means the blending of materialistic goals with spiritual imperatives as the primary goal of economic policy.

M.S. Golwalkar, or affectionately as "Guruji" the organizational genius behind the RSS which is a fervent Hindutva cadre-based volunteer organisation of more than 1+ million, had stated in his *Bunch of Thoughts* (page 5): "All attempts and experiments made so far were based on 'isms' stemming from materialism. However, we Hindus have a solution to offer."

He propounded that "the problem boils down to one of achieving a synthesis of national aspirations and world welfare." Golwalker advocates that in this synthesis, "*swalambana* (or self-reliance) forms the backbone of a free and prosperous nation..." (p.313), and that at the very minimum, "*atma poorti*" (or self-sufficiency) in food production is a must for our national defence..." (p.316).

The difference between *swalambana* and *atma poorti* is this: the former requires that we must depend on our own resources, i.e., if there is a shortage of some commodity, we should earn enough foreign exchange by exports to buy it from abroad.

That is, we should depend on our own resources. The latter concept of *atma poorti* requires that we produce in sufficient quantities in our own country so that we do not suffer in any shortage in any required commodity. That is, we should depend only on our own indigenous production.

Today obviously that is not the situation in India. We find that the nation has moved from food self-sufficiency (*atma poorti*) in the mid-seventies to dependence on imports from abroad.

Golwalker's warning thus was timely. India must re-orient the objective of our economic policy to re-gain self-sufficiency in food production, and must do it by environmental friendly means such as organic farming, wind energy, and cooperative endeavour.

Upadhyaya thus brought out how the objective of economic policy is different from the objective in foreign ideologies of Capitalism, Socialism and Communism. He propounded therefore the concept of 'Integral Man' as assimilating and harmonizing the *chaturvidha purushartha* [four energies] which he elaborated as a concept in his Integral Humanism.

He added the concept of *Chiti*, the soul of the nation, which each nation must discover to decide the correct formulation of economic policy. The concept of *Chiti* of a nation is an original contribution of Upadhyaya, but a more articulate version is the concept of identity elaborated by the late Harvard Professor, Samuel Huntington in his book *Who Are We?*.

Upadhyaya's stress on the need to think in integrated terms is now fashionably called "systems analysis or holistic view" in the West. He also emphasized the need to liberate man by recognizing "complementarities" in life, which in a narrower economic context is 'external economies' or social cost-benefit analysis.

The human is not on his own, or alone. His plea for rejection of class struggle and the need to think in terms of conflict resolution and "class harmony" is now much in vogue today in the West—which is getting increasingly disillusioned with capitalism. In the same vein, Guruji ridiculed the Communist concept of 'dictatorship of the proletariat.' He said it is actually "dictatorship of the dictator of a dictatorial party" [p.13]. How true!

If we are not to suffer the societal unhappiness and tensions of the West, then we have to break away from the path that we have chosen presently, viz., the Nehruvian materialistic path that needs to be completely abandoned. Partially is not enough for national good. The alternative to materialistic capitalism is not communism because even in Communist countries, there is a problem of "alienation" and "exploitation" as revealed recently from reports that have been received.

Deendayal Upadhyaya was also aware as early as in 1965, of the Communist degeneration. Logically for him, any system in which man does not receive primacy is bound to ultimately degenerate. Interestingly Deendayalji quotes M. Djilas the author of *The New Class* to prove that in Communist countries, "a new class of bureaucratic exploiter has come into existence."

Thus, by presenting his Integral Humanism, Deendayal Upadhyaya has placed before the world a new original alternative ideological framework. To appreciate the fundamentally different structure of economic policy imbedded in Integral Humanism, I have below in tabular form for ready reference, placed the various alternative competing ideologies in terms of its structural parameters of objectives, priorities, development strategy, resource mobilization, and institutional framework.

From the table we may note that the economic perspective of Integral Humanism is fundamentally different from the other ideologies. Capitalism and communism have similarities in matters of objectives and institutional framework. If cost of production is stabilized, then maximum profit and maximum production are identical.

Again, class struggle and annihilation and survival of fittest, are different only to the extent that communism envisages the survival of the "fittest" class, whereas capitalism expects the "fittest" individual to engage in fierce competition and annihilate the other rivals. Similarly, socialism has only a difference of degree with communism—on the extent of coercion and control, and not fundamentally. That is why communism is often referred to as "scientific" socialism, although there is nothing scientific about it.

Since one socialism differs from another socialism only in degrees, therefore there are unlimited varieties of socialism varying from those of Hitler's Nazism, Uganda's Idi Amin's, Indira Gandhi's, to democratic socialism of Sweden. This has only caused confusion—and gives ample scope to hypocrisy. Thus we can see some people in India arguing on one hand for nationalization and austerity, and at the same time encouraging foreign collaboration while living in mansions. Such inconsistencies can be reconciled in some variety of socialism, interpreted at will.

From the above table it is also apparent that total humanity and growth, of man is nowhere under consideration in any ideology except in Integral Humanism. Humanity as a whole is in subservient to these systems either explicitly or implicitly. Under communism, man explicitly subserves the system. Coercion is legitimized "in the interest of the State." Even the choice of a career, location of work, and advancement are strictly directed by the State. Man in such countries has no room for choice or even any option to opt out of such a system because his freedom to travel out of the country is also completely curbed.

In capitalism, an individual may have technical freedom for his "pursuit of happiness," but the system fails to accommodate the varying capabilities and endowments of man. Since the law of the jungle ... the survival of the fittest ... prevails, therefore some achieve great advancement while others get trampled and disabled in what is called the "rat race." Since maximum profit is possible only in a newer and latest technology, man has to adjust to the terrifying demands of technology, rather than technology adjusting to the integral needs of man. So we witness today in an advanced capitalist country such as USA, broken homes, high divorce rates and ruined family life have become common because technology has run riot there in making these eruet demands. So man has to adjust to it or perish. Such a development is inevitable in a system in which the "shortage of manpower (is) the guiding factor in the design of machines."

Thus in capitalism, under laissez faire, although man has technical freedom, but because the development strategy is to give primacy to technology, therefore implicitly man becomes subservient to the system. In such societies individuality is thus expressed in other outlets as crime, free sex, drunkenness, and rebel dropout movements. The recent craze in the West for our "Sadhus" and Hindu religion arises largely due to this search for individuality, to escape the mental tensions which this kind of technology demands from the people, and because their own religious preachers are ill-equipped to cope with it.

Just as survival of the fittest is dehumanizing, so is class struggle which is the foundation of Marxism. Under communism, classes are sought to be eliminated by the intensification of class struggle. Obviously such intensification will lead to hate and tension, consequently dehumanization. We saw the extent of such dehumanization in communist countries, In the USSR, for example, most prominent intellectuals such as Alexander Solzenitsyn, Andrie Sakharov had suffered severe punishment from the state because they had questioned this dehumanizating process.

I need not dwell any further on the demerits of other ideologies, but consider in, concrete positive terms, what economic perspectives Hindutva offers. I would organize these first in terms of basic economic postulates using modern theoretical terminology and jargon.

Postulate 1: The economy is a sub-system of the society and not the sole guiding factor of social growth. Hence no economic theorems can be formulated without first recognising that life is an integral system, and therefore whatever economic laws are deduced or codified, they must add or at least not reduce the integral growth of man. The centrality of Man's divine spark and his evolution is on the four Chaturvidha Purusharthas of dharma, artha, kama, moksha.

Postulate 2: There is plurality, and diversity in life. Man is subject to several internal contradictions. The solution is to be based on the harmonization of this plurality, diversity, and internal contradictions. Thus laws governing this harmony will have to be discovered and codified, which we shall call Dharma. An economy based on Dharma will be a. regulated one, within which man's personality and freedom will be given maximum scope, and be enlightened in the social interest.

Postulate 3: There is a negative correlation between the State's coercive power and Dharma. In the latter, the acceptance of regulation by man is voluntary because it blends with his individual and collective aspirations, whereas in the former regulations often conflict with aspirations and hence man is coerced to accept the regulation or suffer.

Postulate 4: A society of persons of common origin, history or culture has a chiti (soulforce). It is this chiti which integrates and establishes harmony. Each nation has to search out its chiti and recognise it consciously. Consequently, each country must follow its own development strategy based on its chiti. If it tries to duplicate or replicate other nations, it will come to grief.

Postulate 5: Based on the perception of chiti and recognition of dharma, an economic order can be evolved which rationalizes the mutual inter-balances of the life system, by seeking out the complementarities embedded in various conflicting interests in society. Such an order will reveal the system of social choices based on an aggregation of individual values.

Postulate 6: Any economy based on Integral Humanism, will take as given, besides the normal democratic fundamental rights, the Right to Food, the Right to Work, Right to Education, and the Right to Free Medical Care as basic rights.

Postulate 7: The right to property is not fundamental, but economic regulation will be based on the complementarity that exists in the conflicting goals of social ownership of property and the necessity for providing incentive to save and to produce.

These seven postulates represent the foundation of the Integral Humanism economic policy. Most of the established and popular slogans of Indian society emanate from one or more (in combination) of these postulates.

For example, the electrifying call of the Freedom Movement for Swadeshi, or self-reliance is embedded in Postulate 4. The popular demand for decentralization finds its source in Postulate 3.

The modern internationally fashionable slogan of environment and pollution control follows from Postulate 5.

The widespread scientific consensus that optimum solutions can only be found in "systems analysis" is contained explicitly in Postulate 1.

Mahatma Gandhi's advocacy of Trusteeship is implied in Postulates 2 and 7 read together. In other words, these seven postulates can singly or jointly conceptualize and synthesize the various goals which have stirred the soul of India (or its chiti).

With these postulates, we now need to derive the practical guidelines for our economic development. To do that, postulate 5 is very important.

First and foremost, we shall have to list out the various complementarities, second, work out a calculus of costs and benefits to integrate these various complementarities; and third, frame decision rules on how to make social choices based on divergent individual values.

An example of complementarities is that of an orchard farmer who has as his neighbour a honey producer. The bees of the honey producer can conveniently utilize the fruit blossoms of the orchard farmer with no cost to either but gain to both. This is an example of positive complementarity.

An example of negative complementarity is that of pollution. For example, by setting up a fertilizer plant and oil refinery on an extensive scale employment in that area is certainly generated. But the toxic gases released by these factories adversely affect the health of the public and reduce the productivity of the workers of the entire region. So overall, the nation is the loser.

We have to select positive complementarities and eschew the negative ones, if Integral Humanism is to be followed. Therefore, we have to plan our urban habitation system in such a way that toxic creating machines are kept far from urban residential centres, or subject to strict environmental measures such as requiring CNG instead of diesel run public transportation buses.

This means our transportation system will have to be integrated in location planning of industries as well. A good capitalist or a communist will look at the problem piece-meal. The capitalist would choose urban centres because profits are highest there.

A Communist would also pick urban centres because production will be maximum where a trained, industrial labour force resides, and an infrastructure is available. In a capitalist society, the "survival of the fittest" is the slogan so there are no complementarities to worry about.

In a communist society, the State is so powerful and coercive that no one questions its decision, in a democratic socialist society, the public will make a few noises, so the Government will order a few anti-pollution devices to be installed but urban centres will still be the location in the end.

However in an Integral Humanist society, the outlook will be systems-oriented, so the location would be "optimized," which will not be the urban centre. But a loss in monetary terms would have been suffered to the managers of the enterprise who would have preferred the maximum profit—area of the urban centre.

So a "calculus" of incentives and compensation for effecting the complementarity is needed. Such a calculus is known to economists, but which for shortage of space, I shall not elaborate here. To do that here would make this paper unduly technical and mathematical.

It is not enough to have a calculus to aggregate the complementarities but also to frame decision rules on how to make consistent social choices based on individual values. It is not enough to say that in a democracy, social choices should be based on majority decision rule. The format for eliciting this majority needs to be spelt out, otherwise anamolies will result.

For example, suppose we divide society into three groups - A: Agriculturists, M: Manufacturers, S: Workers and those in services. Let us assume that the society consisting of A, M, and S has to rank the projects of X; Fertilizer plant; Y: Steel mill; and Z: Hospital, in order of preference. Thus agriculturists (A) will rank X most important of all, Y second most important, and Z as least important. Therefore a choice is offered to them between X and Y, they would choose X. If a choice is between Y and Z, then Y will be chosen. Obviously if X is preferred to Y, and Y is preferred to Z, then X will of course be preferred to Z for consistency. In notation, I shall write: '→' for 'preferred to'

Assume: A: X→ Y→ Z
M: Y→ Z→ X
S: Z→ X→ Y

If a vote is taken on each pairs of projects, then we shall have:

X→Y	A+S=2	M=1	X→Y i.e., choose X over Y
Y→Z	A+M=2	S=1	Y→Z i.e., choose Y over Z
X→Z	A=1	M+S=2	Z→X i.e., choose Z over X

This, in a majority decision without any format, a society may prefer with 2/3 majority, X over Y, Y over Z, and yet prefer over X ! To avoid such social inconsistency, we must ensure that A, M, and S consult each other and seek to find out their complementarity in choices, and then vote.

This is why format and creation of a basic consensus or harmony is so essential. Such a process is lengthy, cumbersome, and complicated. But this is the only way to optimize the nation's energies. But the process can be simplified by decentralization of political and economic authority. It cannot be achieved in a centralized society.

Once a decision is taken on the path of development, Deendayalji would advocate incentives, and realistic taxation to encourage saving, and to discourage conspicuous consumption as the only practical way to mobilize resources. This is contained in postulate 7. Most ideologies are weak when it comes to specifying resource mobilization, perhaps, because spelling it out means annoying one section or another. Therefore, the topic is either handled in a general way or indirectly. In Hindu way of life man must be encouraged to save, live simply and acquire wealth, but then it must be made socially prestigious to give away his wealth or manage it as a "trustee" for society. In western societies, the size of a person's wealth is the most important determinant of his social, cultural and national prestige. So he is encouraged to part with a portion of his wealth by urging him to spend more and on himself! This results in a fierce competition on who can spend more on himself "keeping up with the Joneses" leading to great waste.

In Integral Humanism's scheme of things, social and cultural influences are integrated into a man's psyche, so that parting with his wealth for society becomes his own desire. In such a framework, there is no weakening of a person's resolve to have his income or pursue its immediate enlargement. Philanthropy is an essentially pillar of democracy, and hence as Mahatma Gandhi had said, the rich must treats themselves as trustees of the nation's wealth.

CHAPTER 6

Hindutva-Based Governance

The world has come around to the view that democracy is essential for full human development which is possible only through education and skill development. The view of the late Singapore President Lee Kuan Yew, at one end and Communists at the other, that economic development must be first achieved before democracy is possible, has now been decisively rejected.

But democracy cannot be sustained unless the electorate is well informed, chooses its leadership wisely and the leadership chosen is intellectually empowered by a multi-dimensional intelligence.

Since the world view of economic development has completely changed, economic development is no more thought of human labour driven of Karl Marx or as capital-driven of Alfred Marshall, but now as knowledge-driven.

The world has seen three main ideologies in the nineteenth and twentieth centuries. These are Capitalism, Communism, and Democratic Socialism. The United States, the U.K. and some West European countries have practiced Capitalism. The USSR was a prominent Communist country and China remains one. Scandinavian nations have adopted Democratic Socialism. All three are inappropriate and unsuitable for Indian identity.

All three ideologies are one-dimensional and materialist in character. Although through them, some nations have been able to raise the standards of living of their peoples, the countries adopting these ideologies have failed to make their people happy.

In the United States and Europe, the economic prosperity achieved has been admired by all, but the social problems created in the process have begun to raise serious questions about whether the achieved economic growth is worth the price paid by society.

The movement for environmental protection, anti-pollution measures etc., have all meant putting a brake on this kind of growth. But more surprising is the rise in the number of people in these countries who are becoming adherents of spiritual practices such as meditation and Yoga, and are adopting *gurus* from India.

A certain consensus is taking shape all over the world that material progress has to blend with spiritual values to make national development meaningful to the people. This the age-old contribution of Hindu civilization.

Pure material progress produces new kinds of exploitation replacing the old degeneration of human decencies, leading to a "rat race." On the other hand a purely spiritually minded society is not a viable concept. Society needs to eat and live tolerably well.

Material progress is thus necessary, but it must not be an end in itself. Therefore a blend is necessary, between pursuit of material progress and the adherence to spiritual and moral values. This should be our goal in renaissance or what in India we call as *sanatana dharma*.

It is generally assumed by our English-educated elite that the prevalent system of Government in ancient India was monarchy. The view is based on the assumption that since there were kings in ancient India, therefore system was monarchy. A deeper look suggests that the system in ancient India was more akin to a republic than a monarchy, though it was neither in essence.

Perhaps the closest of the current systems is constitutional monarchy or much like India's ceremonial presidency. Anil Chawla, an activist based on Bhopal, has made a deep study of Republics of Ancient India. Here I rely on his studies. First two definitions:

Oxford English Dictionary defines *Republic* as follows:

1. A state in which the supreme power rests in the people and their elected representatives or officers, as opposed to one governed by a king or similar ruler; a commonwealth. Now also applied loosely to any state which claims this designation.

On the other hand *Monarchy* is defined as follows:

2. A state having a form of government in which the supreme power is vested in a single person. Formerly, also, a nation or state having dominating power over all other states. absolute or despotic m absolute or despotic m., a government by the absolute will of the monarch. constitutional m. (see constitutional a. 4 b). elective m., one in which the monarch is determined by election as opposed to heredity. hereditary m., one in which the sovereign power descends by hereditary right.

Thus, a *Republic* involves *just one distinguishing condition*—the supreme power does not rest with any single individual. While *Monarchy* is based on the concept that the *Sovereign power of the Crown is supreme*. In a monarchy, the King's will is final, without any 'advice' from any person or body acting as a control or check on the King.

Moreover in governance of a country involves three institutions—Legislature, Judiciary and Executive, the King is the head of all three institutions.

The King is the law-maker as well as the ultimate judge and is responsible for executive functions. On the other hand, the distinction between the three institutions is an essential feature of Republics. The supreme power which rests in the people and their elected representatives or officers in a republic is exercised through these institutions which are supposed to maintain an arm's length distance among themselves. In a monarchy, the Crown's will being Supreme, the distinction between the three institutions (if at all present) gets blurred since a single individual acts as the head of all three.

To understand the systems prevalent at that time, it is interesting to look at the nature and origin of Hindu Law about which John Mayne said in July, 1878 "Hindu Law has the oldest pedigree of any known system of jurisprudence, and even now it shows no signs of decrepitude. At this day it governs races of men, extending from Cashmere to Cape Comorin, who agree in nothing else except their submission to it."

It should be noted that the British who have always (erroneously) prided themselves on uniting India were forced to admit that even after almost eight centuries of foreign rule, the country "from Cashmere to Cape Comorin" was governed by a common set of laws and this was when the country was said to have been divided into hundreds of small kingdoms. Contrast this with Europe where there have never been more than a handful of countries (say maximum fifty countries) and yet there has never been a common set of laws. Each European King made his own laws and his freedom in this respect was said to be the concept of 'sovereignty'.

The situation in India was very different because no King had any legislative powers in ancient India. Legislative activity or Law making was done only at the Centres of Learning which can well be called the Universities of that time. Varanasi, Ujjain, Nalanda, Rameshwaram and almost all major temple towns were such centres of learning.

The word Rishi used in Indian texts has often been translated as ascetic or sage but this creates a confusion and lends to the term a super-human aura, a sort of mysticism. An impression has often been created in public mind that the Rishis who framed laws did nothing else but sit meditating under a tree or in some cave in Himalayas. Nothing can be more removed from truth. Almost all rishis were married and lived a healthy family life. The best comparison of a rishi can be to the modern day university professor who lives in his university campus far removed from the din of the city and devotes himself to intellectual pursuits.

Laws in ancient India were codified in Smritis. It is interesting to look at Mayne's view in regard to Hindu law—"According to Hindu conception, law in the modern sense was only a branch of Dharma, a word of the widest import and not easily rendered into English. Dharma includes religious, moral, social and legal duties and can only be defined by its contents.

The Mitakshara mentions the six divisions of Dharma in general with which the Smritis deal; and the divisions relate to the duties of the castes, the duties of orders of ASRAMAS, the duties of orders of particular castes, the special duties of kings and others, the secondary duties which are enjoined for transgression of prescribed duties; and the common duties of all men. [Mitakshara on Yajn. I, 1 (Setlur's Edn., p4); Varnadharma, asramadharma, varnasramadharma, gunadharma, nimittadharma and sadharanadharma....]" (emphasis added by author).

The interesting feature that is central to our discussion is that the Smritis inter alia provided for the duties of Kings. This obviously implies that any king was governed by the Smritis that were drafted not by himself or by his predecessors but by bodies of intellectuals.

A king was prohibited from becoming a law-maker or even interpreting the law. However after the 10th century, when the invasion of Islam led to a destruction of the famous Universities of India, some kings, as an attempt to safeguard knowledge, either took upon themselves or encouraged their ministers to take up the task of writing Commentaries and Digests of the Smritis. "A commentary on the Code of Manu was written in the 11th century by Dhareshwava or King Bhoja or Dhara in Malwa. A little later, Vijnanesvara wrote his famous Mitakshara on the Smriti of Yajnavalkya under the auspices of King Vikramarka or Vikramaditya of Kalyan in Hyderabad."

Thus, during the period that is classified as ancient in Indian history i.e. upto 1000 AD, Kings and their ministers had neither the power to make any laws nor the power to interpret Laws.

Even after the establishment of the Islamic rule in the country, the Smriti law continued to be fully recognized and enforced because the invader came with near zero skills for governance.

The picture that emerges from the above observations is very different from the image of a King in Europe, where based on the theory of divine power of the King, *'Sovereignty of the Crown is supreme'* and *'A King is always right'* were the well-accepted rules. A ritual that was carried out at the time of coronation of any Hindu King (until very recently) illustrates the position of the King in ancient India. After the coronation, the crowned King declares that he is all powerful.

As soon as he declares his acquired power, the Rajguru (the chosen representative of the rishis) hits him with a Dand (a wooden rod) and tells him that Dharma and not he is the most powerful. The act of hitting him with a Dand is a symbolic punishment to remind him of his subordination to the Law as decided by the intellectual class. This is unimaginable in the coronation of a European King.

While classifying the system as republic, we must keep in mind that a republic need not always be democratic. Fascist and autocratic regimes have also been classified as republics. *Compared to many of the modern day republics, the ancient Indian system was a true republic and classifying it as monarchy is a mistake that social and political scientists must correct without any delay.*

As nature abhors a vacuum, this void is being increasingly filled, using religious symbols India being 83 per cent Hindu, and furthermore since the folklore in this religion has been pan-Indian, it is easy for the masses to understand the religious bonding. Ramayana narration traverses from the Punjab to Srilanka. Mahabharata covers incidents from Assam to Gujarat. Adi Shankara connected Kerala to Kashmir.

The mutilation of Indian history by the British and later by the JNU cabal the absurd Aryan-Dravidian two-nation two race theory propounded by the British had been rejected by all Indian seers and patriots whether it was Swami Vivekananda, or Subramania Bharati, or Dr. Ambedkar. Yet till recently, the Nehru acolytes had assiduously propagated il and incorporated it into school curriculam.

To reject it did not mean that one was a Hindutva fanatic. But was that was what the Nehru secularists precisely alleged. But now it is pathetic to see these very secularists capitulating in the face of recent facts uncovered by new scientific techniques such as DNA testing and lasers. For example, for decades Professor Romila Thapar of JNU propagated the Aryan-Dravidian two race theory.

But in 2002, she has beaten a hasty retreat. In her book: "Penguin History of Early India" she has disowned Aryan-Dravidian race/nation theory altogether! She states now that: "To refer to 'the Aryan' as a race is therefore inaccurate." Better late than never, but it is a pity that she has it after the avalanche of new data and discoveries leaving her no room to hide her bogus scholarship.

Another ancient Hindu value is democracy, embedded in the concept of discussion [shrashtratha], consensus, and tolerance. Hence, Jews, Syrian Christians and Zoroastrians persecuted the world over found a safe sanctuary in India and co-opted into Hindu society while they retained their religious identity. This is the essence of democracy.

And now the world has come around to the view that democracy is essential for full human development which is sustainable only through education and skill development of the youth.

The view of Lee Kuan Yew of Singapore at one end and Communists at the other, that economic development must be first achieved before democracy is possible, has now been decisively rejected.

But democracy cannot be nurtured unless the electorate is intellectually empowered by informed intelligence, which is a multi-dimensional concept, and the electorate chooses its leadership wisely. Further Directive Principles in the Constitution lays down the governance imperatives for the State.

The Supreme Court [in Charu Khanna vs. Union of India AIR 2015 SC 839] holds the Directive Principles laid down in Article 38 to 51 as representing the "soul" of the Constitution of India.

The Constitution also prescribes duties of a citizen under 11 heads and that it is the responsibility of the State to ensure the citizen is encouraged to perform his duties as a part of the soft infrastructure of good governance.

Of these, Article 44 is a Directive Principle for State Policy to secure for the citizens a uniform *civil* code throughout the territory of India.

While there is not much resistance to a uniform civil code and moreover since the Muslims on ground of violation of the Shariat have not objected to a uniform *criminal* code which the Indian Penal Code is, hence it is constitutional to enforce Article 44 as not violative of Article 15.

The question whether India should adopt a uniform civil code should be treated as a legal question because it is a mandate addressed to the 'State' by Art.44 under Directive Principles of the Constitution. Unfortunately, in India, legal questions are politicized when it affects the "Muslim vote bank."

Article 44 of the Constitution says –

"The State shall endeavour to secure for the citizens a uniform civil code throughout the territory of India."

A controversy has however arisen as to the formation of a uniform code relating to the family or personal law of the parties relating to matters such as marriage and divorce, succession, adoption.

The framers of the Constitution clearly indicated what they meant by the word 'personal law' in Entry 5 of List III of the 7th Schedule of the same Constitution:

Entry 5 says:

"5. Marriage and divorce; infants and minors; adoption; wills; intestacy and succession; joint family and partition; all matters in respect of which parties in judicial proceedings were immediately before the commencement of this Constitution subject to their personal law."

The makers of the Constitution had witnessed the baneful effects of a claim for separate identity of the Muslim community such as separate electorate on the ground that their religion, laws prescribed a separate Personal Law, resulting in the lamentable Partition of India on the footing of the theory of 'two Nations', founded on two religions.

The debate in the House of Commons UK on the Indian Independence Act to legitimize the Partition held in June-July 1947 makes clear that the object of the Bill introduced was to create "a Muslim governed Pakistan and a Hindu governed India."

But the then Congress Party resolved after Partition that the Indian State would be secular, which is consistent with the Hindu ethos but did not require to be made a Constitutional principle. But over the decades since 26 January 1950 when the Constitution became effective, Congress' electoral politics eroded and distorted definition of secularism and changed to religious minority appeasement.

Hence, in the Constituent Assembly it was made clear that in a secular State personal laws relating to such matters as marriage, succession and inheritance could not depend upon religion, but must rest on the law of the land. A uniform Civil Code was accordingly necessary for achieving the unity and solidarity of the nation. [K.M. Munshi, VII C.A.D., 547-48].

Every time subsequently the question of uniform Civil Code was raised by anyone in Parliament, the Government of India opposed it on the ground that to achieve it would be to hurt Muslim 'sentiments' and that no implementation of this Directive of the fundamental law could be made so long as the

Muslims themselves would not come forward to ask for it. Nevertheless, the Supreme Court has recommended, more than once, to take early steps towards the formation of a uniform Civil Code [Mudgal v. Union of India (1995) 3 S.C.C. 635—Kuldip Singh and Sahai JJ. (10 May, 1995)].

That the Shariat is not infallible or immutable is evidenced by the patent fact that it has been discarded on modified in many respects by various Muslim States. And this has been achieved in an orthodox Muslim State such as Tunisia, through the process of liberal or progressive interpretation of the scriptures.

That the Shariat on personal law is not sacrosanct will appear from the following examples of Muslim majority countries which have superseded or modified polygamy.

Turkey: The Court can declare a second marriage as invalid on the ground that a spouse is living at the time of the second marriage [Turkish Civil Code, Art. 74].

Pakistan: A person cannot contract a second marriage without the permission of the Arbitration Council; and a wife can obtain divorce on the ground that the husband has married another wife.

Iran: A person cannot remarry without permission of the Court.

Egypt, Jordan, Morocco, Syria: Similar restrictions on bigamy as in Iran and Pakistan have been imposed in Egypt, Jordan, Morocco and Syria.

Tunisia: Bigamy is totally prohibited by the Tunisia Law of personal Status (s. 18).

Registration of all marriages, including those contracted in conformity with Shariat formalities, has been made compulsory in Iran, Algeria, Indonesia, Malaysia.

There is no reason why such law cannot be adopted in India.

Advocates of immutability should be silenced by the following observations of a Judge of Pakistan, Huq, J., of the Lahore High Court:

"it would not be correct to lay it down as a positive rule of law that the present-day Courts in this country should have no power or authority to interpret the Quran in a way different from that adopted by the earlier Jurists and Imams. The adoption of such a view is likely to endanger the dynamic and universal character of the religion and laws of Quran."

The ground of immutability of the Shariat was in fact raised by some Muslim members in the Constituent Assembly of India but was rejected on the opposition from Dr. Ambedkar. It would be an eyeopener to many today to recount what Ambedkar said [VII C.A.D. 55] in this context.

"... up to 1935 the North-West Frontier Province was not subject to Shariat Law; it followed the Hindu Law in the matter of succession and in other matters, so much so that it was in 1939 that the Central Legislature had to come into the field and to abrogate the application of the Hindu Law to Muslims of North-West Frontier Province and to apply Shariat Law to them ... apart from North-West Frontier Province, up till 1937 in the rest of India, in various parts, such as the United Provinces, the Central Provinces and Bombay, the Muslims to a large extent were governed by the Hindu Law in the matter of succession ... that in North-Malabar the Marumakkathayam law applied to all—not only to Hindus but also to Muslims." [op. cit]

Even in India the Koranic laws of crimes and evidence have been supplanted as early as the 19th century by enacting the Penal Code and the Evidence Act, e.g., by saving the Muslims from the following mediaeval atrocities which are still prevalent in Muslim countries like Pakistan and Bangladesh.

In this context, it has to be pointed out that in Goa, from the days of Portuguese rule, the people have been governed by a uniform civil code, and that Goanese Muslims have not lost their identity or culture because of that.

If it is contended that personal law, founded on religion, has any special status, the answer is that it is the British Parliament which made the English Crown the head of the Church and altered the law of royal succession; and an Indian Parliament superseded the Hindu law of marriage and succession, in the teeth of opposition from an enlightened section of Hindus.

It was opposed by Dr. Rajendra Prasad himself on the grounds that Art.44, being applicable to all persons in the territory of India, should not be imposed on the Hindus alone and that the Government who sponsored the Hindu Code Bill to replace the personal law of the Hindus had no mandate from the Electorate in this behalf.

Above all, the Muslims who remained in India after the Partition did so with the full knowledge that divided India was going to adopt a Parliamentary system of democracy and not any Muslim system of the Middle Ages where Shariat would be the supreme law of the land.

They should also have known that a personal law founded on the religion of different communities was incompatible with the very concept of a 'Secular' State which divided India was going to be.

The Supreme Court can no more wash its hands off Art. 44 on the ground that it is a Directive Principle which is not directly enforceable [Jordan v. Chopra (1985) 3 S.C.C 62]. Article 37 of the Constitution ensures that.

Thus, Hindutva Governance is defined in, and circumscribed by the Constitution, and draws its road map from the Directive Principles and Rights and Duties enshrined in the Constitution.

CHAPTER 7

Conclusions

The Ideology of the Modern Right as discussed in preceding chapters is summarized thus as Virat Hindutva, and is constituted in five dimensions as noted below.

1. The Correct Identity of an Indian

An Indian is either a Hindu, or if not a Hindu, those others who acknowledge (as modern genetic research on DNA of Indians reveals) that their ancestors are Hindus. All others are Indian citizens.

Brahmins, Kshatriya, Vaishya, Shudra, Scheduled Castes and Tribals of India all show a common genetic ancestry. The age of this yet- to- be- determined common parentage goes back, in India itself, to at least 9,000 years and possibly even earlier than 20,000 years ago, leaving no scientific genetic support for recent British Imperialist sponsored migration theories, including the concocted Aryan-Dravidian theory.

Hence the Hindustani in the present day and age has the same DNA irrespective of varna, region, religion, and language.

2. The De-falsified History of India

A truthful factual History records that we Indians are one ethnic people from North to South, and East to West of India and not a product of a mass immigration from other parts of the world.

It detailsthe Hindu relentless struggle against invading Islamic hordes from abroad which made Hindustan unique having never capitulated to these maraudering hordes, thus explaining why India is still 80% even after 800 years of Islamic Rule in India, unlike Persia, Iraq and Egypt which were Islamised within 25 years.

3. Economic Theory of Integral Humanism

This Economic ideology requires shifting our focus from purely materialistic theory of capitalism, socialism and communism to an integral view of material progress harmonized with spiritual values. Modern economic growth also is powered overwhelmingly (over 65% of GDP) by new innovation and techniques (e.g., internet). More capital and labour contributes less than 35% of growth in GDP. This requires a disciplined intellectual focus of the younger generation. Universities are green houses for our youth to find their roots and develop and flower their intelligence for pursuit of their chosen careers after graduation and to live a good family life in a vibrant democracy. Unfortunately the educational system we have today is the same as designed by Macaulay in 1835, with intention to produce civil servants and clerks for the British to rule over the Indian masses.

4. Sanskrit as the national link language

In the centuries to come, it is Sanskrit that will be the most sensible link language for us Indians. There are two reasons for it. The first is that all Indian languages have a high proportion of words taken from Sanskrit. In the case of Bengali and Malayalam it may be 85 per cent, while in the case of Tamil it is at least 35 per cent (even in the DMK version of "pure" Tamil).

Bengali is proudly referred to as the "daughter" of Sanskrit, but Tamil which has a proud history of its own, thanks to the long unbroken reign of the Chola and Pandyan kingdoms, is thought of as the "sister" of Sanskrit since Tamil is almost as old as Sanskrit.

For this reason, Sanskritized Hindi is easier to understand for the Southerners because of the substantial common vocabulary Hence Sanskrit is ultimately the best national language for India.

Further, international research in today's most advanced area of computers, namely, Artificial Intelligence, which is to revolutionize the knowledge systems of the 21st Century, is now increasingly coming to the conclusion that Sanskrit is the best language to store knowledge in a computer. Dr. Rick Briggs of the US National Aeronautics and Space Agency (NASA), in an article in *Journal of Artificial Intelligence* (1968), titled *Knowledge Representation in Sanskrit and Artificial Intelligence* that: "In the past twenty years, much time, effort, money has been expended on designing an unambiguous representation of natural languages to make them accessible to computer processing.... There is at least one language, Sanskrit ... (in which) can be reckoned a method ... that is identical not only in essence but in form with current work in Artificial Intelligence. This article demonstrates that a natural language (Sanskrit) can serve as an artificial language also, and that much work in Artificial Intelligence has been reinventing a wheel millenia old."

5. Virat Hindutva Mindset and Governance

It is the commitment of 'zero tolerance' for terrorists, also for those who forcibly or by inducements seek to convert Hindus to other religion, and to never negotiate with them unless they surrender, and to retaliate against the political objectives of these enemies. Retaliation must be massive enough to deter future attacks on us. Thus, Virat Hindutva minded Indians must prefer to lose everything they possess rather than submit to treachery, tyranny or to terrorism.

On these five pillars rests the new Ideology of the Right which is constitutionally compliant and is modern in perspective.